MONS

MONS
THE RETREAT TO VICTORY

John Terraine

WORDSWORTH EDITIONS

ACKNOWLEDGEMENTS

The Information contained in this book is drawn from many sources, and the author is conscious of the debt that he owes to all of them. A special mention must, however, be made of the following works which provided the foundation on which all else rests: *The Official History of the War* compiled by Brig-Gen. J. E. Edmonds; *Liaison, 1914* by Sir Edward Spears; the *Memoirs of Marshal Joffre; 1914* by the Earl of Ypres; *Memories of Forty-Eight Years Service* by General Sir Horace Smith-Dorrien; *The War in the Air* by Walter Raleigh; *The Wilson Diaries* edited by Maj-Gen. Sir C. E. Callwell; and *Alarms and Excursions* by Lieut-Gen. Sir Tom Bridges.

The Author and Publishers wish to thank the following for permission to include the illustrations appearing in this book:
Historisches Bildarchiv, Handke, Bad Berneck, for figs. 14-18. The Imperial War Museum, for figs. 1-3, 5, 7, 13, 21, 23, 24 and 28-31. F.Matania Esq, for fig. 32. The Curator, The Middlesex Regimental Museum, for fig. 33. La Musé de l'Armé, Paris, for fig.11. Radio Time Hulton Picture Library, for figs. 4, 6, 8 and 9. Major-General Sir Edward Louis Spears, K.C.B., C.B., M.C., F.Inst.D., for figs. 12 and 27 (from *Liaison, 1914* – Heinemann, 1930). Ullstein Bilderdienst, Berlin, for figs. 19 and 22. Figs. 10, 20, 25 and 26 are from the author's collection

The Author is grateful to all those who drew his attention to errors in the illustrations of the first impression of this book, and believes that these have now been corrected.

First published in Great Britain in 1960
by B. T. Batsford Ltd

Copyright © John Terraine 1960

This edition published 2002
by Wordsworth Editions Limited
Cumberland House, Crib Street, Ware,
Hertfordshire SG12 9ET

ISBN 1 84022 240 9

© Wordsworth Editions Limited 2002

Wordsworth® is a registered trade mark of
Wordsworth Editions Limited

Printed and bound in Great Britain
by Mackays of Chatham plc, Chatham, Kent.

CONTENTS

LIST OF ILLUSTRATIONS

MAPS

To the
Old Contemptibles

"I have seen Sordet's cavalry march through Inchy on the ever of Le Cateau; I have seen the Iron Corps of France march through the square at Ypres; I have seen the 1st Canadian Division marching to St Julien before the gas attack; I have seen Indian troops going into action for the first time on European soil; I have seen the Australians on their way to the attack of Pozières; but I have no remembrance to equal in any way that of the old regiments of the B. E. F. marching to the battle of Mons."

CAPTAIN C. A. L. BROWNLOW, D.S.O., R.F.A.

"Our motto was, 'We'll do it. What is it?'"

LIEUT-GENERAL SIR TOM BRIDGES,
K.C.B., K.C.M.G., D.S.O., LL. D.

MONS

INTRODUCTION

TWICE IN THIS CENTURY a British Expeditionary Force has taken the field in Northern France to fight beside the French Army at the outbreak of a general European war; twice, this Force has marched into Belgium with the French, to repel a German invasion; twice, its operations have commenced with a short conflict, followed immediately by a precipitate retreat; twice, by something bordering upon a miracle, the Expeditionary Force has survived initial disasters and the threat of complete destruction. There the resemblances cease, for the Retreat to Dunkirk in 1940 was the prelude to the Fall of France, and it was not until four years later that a British Army was able to avenge its defeat on French and Belgian soil. In 1914, an interval of only two weeks separated the first encounter with the enemy at Mons, on Sunday, August 23rd, from the counter-stroke on the Marne which began on Sunday, September 6th, and proved to be one of the decisive battles of history, because it meant the collapse of the German War Plan.

No one who lived through the blazing summer of 1940 is ever likely to forget the vivid sense of doom that pervaded the whole of Britain, while the B.B.C. News bulletins and the daily maps in the newspapers unfolded the story of the plunging progress of the Panzers and Stukas across the plains of north-western Europe. The bombing of Rotterdam, the surrender of King Leopold, the encircling of the Maginot Line, the entry into Paris, the French collapse —all these dire events succeeded each other so swiftly that one was half-impelled to believe that some magical force was at work. The demoniac personality of Adolf Hitler helped to promote this belief. It was too much to expect, at that tense juncture, that public opinion could take a longer view, and see in the terrifying success of the blitzkrieg simply the belated fulfilment of a Plan which had failed a quarter of a century earlier, and which, in all its fundamentals, had been devised in 1905. What Hitler had done was, in effect, simply to supply, through mechanical power, the force which was never available in 1914 to consummate the famous Schlieffen Plan.

The Schlieffen Plan was the corollary of the sensational German victory in the war with France in 1870. The harsh peace dictated to France by Bismarck in 1871, in particular the annexation of Alsace and Lorraine, made it as inevitable as human affairs can be that another conflict would arise between the German Empire and her proud, defeated neighbour. The growth of cordial relations between France and Russia, culminating in the military pact of 1894, made it equally inevitable that when this conflict came, Germany would be faced with the dreaded prospect of war on two fronts. This was the penalty of her central position, which nevertheless carried with it certain compensating strategic advantages. It was the purpose of Graf von Schlieffen, who became Chief of the German General Staff in 1891, and held the post until his retirement in 1906, to exploit these advantages in such a way as to offset the dangers, and, if all went well, avoid having to fight two enemies at once.

Von Schlieffen's plan, as he finally evolved it in 1905, was a bold utilisation of the interior lines of communication that were to serve Germany well in both World Wars. In its detail, indeed, it was one of the boldest strategic enterprises ever devised; its central idea was to dispose completely of one enemy before the other could deploy his forces. Calculating upon the slowness of Russian mobilisation, and regarding the astonishingly revived French Army as his most immediate hazard, von Schlieffen determined to hurl, at the very outbreak of war, almost the whole land strength of Germany against France. His belief that, by adopting this intrepid policy, with all its risks, he could overthrow his most dangerous military rival in a sufficiently short time to re-deploy against the ponderous Russian masses, was fortified by the tactical thinking then current in Germany.

The rapid and total defeat of the French Armies in 1870, with the marvellous climax at Sedan, where Napoleon III surrendered at the head of his whole field force, had set an example of what might be done by boldness and professional skill. Could this wonder be repeated? Von Schlieffen and his colleagues on the General Staff believed that it could. For years, they had been seeking a formula for decisive victory; now they believed that they had discovered it—in Hannibal's triumph at Cannae in 216 B.C. The Carthaginian general's envelopment and destruction of a superior Roman army in that far-off year seemed to point the way to the kind of success that Germany needed in her twentieth-century trial. The difficulty lay in the powerful fortress system that the French had built all along the common frontier. To encircle the French Army, to bring about another Sedan or Cannae, it would be necessary to by-pass this system; this was the consideration that impelled von Schlieffen to plan a march through Belgium.

The violation of Belgian neutrality was the final factor that brought Britain into the War; British thought has consequently tended to dwell upon it. But it was not merely in the march through Belgium that the remarkable quality of the plan resided: it was in the weight of the thrust that von Schlieffen proposed to make with the right wing of the German array. His final plan was truly breathtaking in its daring; ten divisions—only ten—would be left to face Russia; sixty-two divisions would march against France. Of these sixty-two divisions, only eight would be drawn up along the common frontier; the remaining fifty-four, in a vast mass, like a great ball on the end of a chain, would swing past the left of the French line, curve round to the west of Paris, mask the capital, and pin the French armies, *from behind*, against their own fortress system and the Swiss frontier. The final subtlety of the concept lay in the fact that any success gained by the French at the expense of the weak German left would contribute to their own undoing. Von Schlieffen's plan was designed to act, as Captain Liddell Hart has said, "like a revolving door—if a man pressed heavily on one side, the other would swing round and hit him in the back."

With all its sweep, all its audacity and all its cleverness, the Schlieffen Plan contained two weaknesses—one inherent, the other accidental. It is very much a question whether the Imperial German Army ever had the sheer quantitive strength that would be needed to carry out such a mighty manœuvre. Even using Reserve formations, contrary to all military precepts, even with the increased strength available in 1914, the Army was strained beyond its limits by the task imposed on it; we can see now that what was really required was the multiplication of manpower by mechanical force that only became feasible in 1940. In 1914, only the most rigorous adherence to von Schlieffen's basic principles of total concentration at the decisive point on the extreme right wing could have offered any hope of success, and such adherence presupposed that his plan would be carried out by a man who shared his vision—and shared his iron nerve. This prerequisite was not fulfilled.

When von Schlieffen retired in 1906, the appointment of his successor was determined largely by a factor which had already begun to cause damage to the German Army—the vanity of the Kaiser, Wilhelm II, the Supreme War Lord. Strong personalities with independent ideas were at a discount at this stage of his reign; Generaloberst Helmuth von Moltke, the nephew of the great leader of the Franco-Prussian War, was a Staff Officer, and a Court soldier. He did not covet the high office that was thrust upon him; he rightly doubted his ability to fill it. He shrank from the radical conclusions accepted by his predecessor; he permitted his mind to dwell upon the enemy's intentions; he became increasingly dubious of von Schlieffen's emphasis on the right wing, increasingly anxious about the possibility of a deep French advance in Lorraine. In the interval between his taking office and the outbreak of war, he so tinkered with the Schlieffen Plan, without daring positively to abandon it, as to rob it of its central and most fertile concept. His re-distribution of force, while it actually weakened the holding group on the Eastern Front, added strength to the Western only where it could be least effective. By 1914, the proportionate weight of the right wing to the left of the Western Armies had been altered from the six to one settled upon by von Schlieffen to only two to one. What remained was sufficient for a most spectacular opening, but not for the "victory without a tomorrow" which Germany absolutely required.

Even the outward brilliance of the initial German onset might have been severely dimmed had French thinking been half as realistic as the calculations of the German General Staff. But the decades between the humiliating collapse of the Second Empire and the First World War were spent by the French Staff in the vain pursuit of lost glories. They had two tasks to perform, in preparing themselves for *La Revanche*, the reversal of the decision of 1871 which preoccupied the French nation like a silent prayer. They had to find a strategic formula for victory, and they had to rebuild the individual morale of the French soldier. Feverish studies of the period of France's greatest military grandeur finally achieved a synthesis of these two aims. In the cryptic doctrines of the first Napoleon, French soldiers believed that a secret recipe could be found that would be specially suitable to the temperament of the nation and the qualities of the French soldier. After years of painstaking study, they concluded that they had it at last; but, ironically, what they fixed upon was the least subtle, the least rewarding, though perhaps the showiest, of the Napoleonic techniques—the massed onslaught, at the "decisive point", of the big battalions, the great columns of all arms which had won such battles as Friedland and Wagram. The Pyrrhic quality of some of these triumphs was ignored, as were the failures of the same method on other fields, most notably, Waterloo.

All French military thought and training was directed to the revival of the instinct for the offensive which was regarded as the central factor in the strategy of Napoleon I, and which had certainly failed to materialise under Napoleon III. By an all-out, immediate offensive, the French Staff believed they could impose their will upon the enemy from the very opening of the campaign, giving him no chance to develop his own plans, and keeping him off balance until the moment came when the great mass of Reserve could be thrown in at the decisive point to complete his overthrow. It was a very simple idea, but its simplicity was not that of strength. It failed to take into account three factors which ought to have been regarded as fundamental from the very beginning: the altered conditions of twentieth-century warfare; the German Plan; the strength of the German Army. It seems inconceivable that otherwise sensible, professional men could neglect such considerations; yet it was so. The reasons were largely psychological. The adoption of this stark theory took its place in the rebuilding of French national morale after catastrophe; it also took its place in the rebuilding of the Army. To implement such a doctrine as this, what was required was to persuade the French soldier that he was personally so superior to his enemy that all he needed to do was to hurl himself forward, and the battle would be won. This was the theme of all French tactical training in the pre-war years; how well it succeeded, and with what disastrous results, will be shown in the pages that follow. But three reflections should temper our criticisms of this crude dogma: first, the fact that French morale *was* sufficiently restored to survive even the calamities that ensued—a point which no one belonging to the generation of 1940 can ignore; secondly, on the material side, the

French were by no means so backward—their field artillery and aviation were particularly well developed; thirdly, their demeanour made its unquestionable impression on their enemies, and was largely responsible for von Moltke's fatal re-shaping of the Schlieffen Plan.

By 1914, French thought had hardened out into a formal plan of operations—the notorious Plan XVII. All their illusions are summed up in its opening paragraphs:

> "From a careful study of information obtained it is probable that a great part of the German forces will be concentrated on the common frontier. . . .
> "Whatever the circumstances, it is the C.-in-C.'s intention to advance, all forces united, to the attack of the German armies. . . ."

With the methods of Napoleon I, then, the French were planning to deliver their attack on the battlefields of Napoleon III, the lost provinces of Alsace and Lorraine. Even beyond the outbreak of the War itself, official Staff thinking remained obstinately blind to the possibilities both of a German advance through Belgium and of its being conducted in enormous strength.

It remains now to consider the role of the small British Regular Army in the inevitable clash of these continental giants. Britain, in 1914, was primarily a sea-power, the greatest in the world, reposing upon a century of supremacy that was only now being challenged. For it was the German Kaiser's fleet-building, more than anything else, that drew Britain into the military Entente with France, and into the morasses of continental politics. The building of the High Seas Fleet was a gesture that could point in only one direction, while the twentieth-century revolution in naval design, which brought sudden obsolescence to the greater part of existing fleets, made the threat particularly menacing. The Royal Navy embarked upon a period of furious re-equipment which so absorbed its energies that, until the Agadir Crisis exposed the weakness, the Admiralty paid almost no attention to global strategic problems.

The Army, on the other hand, as the Entente consolidated, and understanding of French requirements grew, found itself thrust into a position of unwonted prominence. All its weaknesses—and they were many—had been exposed in South Africa. Succeeding Governments were clear that reform was needed, although Army Reform was never a glamorous undertaking in those unmartial days. When the Liberals came to power in 1906, the process received a new impetus. This was the more extraordinary since the Liberal Party was thoroughly permeated with pacifism, and entertained the deepest distrust of militarism in all its forms. But the new Liberal Secretary of State for War, Mr. (later Lord) Haldane, brought to completion, during his remarkable tenure of office, three major steps which transformed the Army: an up-to-date General Staff was firmly lodged in control; an Expeditionary Force was organised; the Territorial Army was created.

Haldane was the greatest War Secretary that Britain has ever had. His philosophical bent and legal training enabled him to approach his task from first principles: "What is the Army for? What will be its future role?" were his questions. The answer he received from the General Staff, and accepted in the absence of any cogently-presented alternative from the naval side, was: "To fight beside the French Army in the event of German aggression". It was to this end that all his work was directed; it was for this purpose that the Regular Army at home was re-organised into an Expeditionary Force of six infantry divisions and a cavalry division, and the Territorials brought into being to replace the Regulars in all their normal duties and to supplement them in the field.

The man most responsible for the strategic thinking that underlay the Haldane Reforms was the ardently Francophile Irishman, Henry Wilson.* From 1907 until 1910, Wilson held the influential post of Commandant of the Staff College; from 1910 until the outbreak of war he held the even more important position of Director of Military Operations at the War Office. It was during his tenure at the Staff College that his close acquaintance with, and deep respect for French ideas and methods began. In 1909, he paid a momentous visit to Paris, and struck up a lasting friendship with his opposite number at the Ecole Supérieure de Guerre, General Foch, one of the great teachers of the offensive school. Foch's influence upon Wilson was profound from the first, and was constantly refreshed by their frequent meetings and long conversations. At one of the earliest of these they discussed German strategy: "His appreciation of the German move through Belgium is exactly the same as mine,"

* Later Field-Marshal Sir Henry Wilson, Bart., G.C.B., D.S.O.

Wilson wrote in his diary, "the important line being between Verdun and Namur." This was written in December, 1909; they both under-estimated German enterprise, but as the War came nearer, they became even more mistaken, and their errors were amplified in the higher Commands of their two Armies.

As Director of Military Operations, it was Wilson's task to prepare for the concentration of the British Army in an agreed zone on French soil, at a stated time. The Staff understanding was that both Armies should mobilise simultaneously, and the British Expeditionary Force should move at once to a position on the left flank of the French; the area selected for its assembly was around Maubeuge. This idea, once settled, assumed the force of a sacred text for Wilson. In 1911, on one of his periodical visits to France and to the battle-fields of 1870, he went, as usual, to Mars-la-Tour. He wrote in his diary: "We paid my usual visit to the statue of 'France', looking as beautiful as ever, so I laid at her feet a small bit of map I have been carrying, showing the areas of concentration of the British forces on her territory." It was an odd procedure on many counts—not least that of security. But its significance lay in the fact that when war came, Wilson's plan for the British Army was the only one in existence; the entire complicated mechanism for mobilising the Army and bringing the nation into a state of war, worked out in extraordinary and impressive detail, was directed to assembling the Expeditionary Force as rapidly as possible at Maubeuge, to join in the great French attack.

War came in July and August, 1914. The Central Powers declared war on Serbia on July 28th, on Russia on August 1st, on France on August 3rd, on Belgium on August 4th, and on Britain on November 23rd; France declared war on August 3rd, and Britain on August 4th. The effective interval was, however, longer than it seemed, for although the Navy had gone straight to its battle stations from the July manoeuvres of the Fleet, the Army did not actually mobilise until after the declaration of war, whereas France mobilised on August 1st. The delay was productive of much ill-feeling between the two countries, and much subsequent confusion. But once the decision was taken, the machine perfected by Haldane, and directed by the work of Wilson, moved with immaculate precision to take its place in the greatest catastrophe that has ever overtaken the civilised world. For the British, the first encounter with this catastrophe was Mons.

Part One : Into Battle

I

Departure and Arrival

THE ARMY—what there was of it—was ready. Only in the matters of the higher direction of the War, and of the scale on which it would be conducted, was the legend of British unpreparedness at all accurate. Mobilisation, planned in very thorough detail, and practised beforehand, was completed with smooth efficiency—so much so that the country scarcely knew that it was happening. In the garrison towns, where the barracks and depots of the regiments were, there was plenty of bustle and activity, of course: Reservists reporting, regiments, batteries, and battalions being placed on a war footing, equipment being issued, colours, plate, and all trimmings being stored, transport being organised, farewell celebrations by those who were going, much heart-burning among those who were being left behind, in case they might 'miss the show'—for this was the war that would 'be over by Christmas', and there were few among those Regular soldiers who imagined the long ordeal that was in store.

The Reservists came streaming into their depots from all over the country, and from all walks of civilian life. For many of them, only recently, and perhaps with difficulty, settled in civil occupations, it must have been a shock, and something of a calamity, to be called back to the colours and whirled away to war. For far too many of them, there would be no return, or a return so maimed and broken that life might as well have ended. But the majority accepted the situation with the stoicism and good humour that the British Army is famous for. The news of their recall came to them in a number of ways, in that era before radio had trained people to its own technique of public announcement and response: telegrams and letters summoned most of them, and notices, too, played their part. The writer Frank Richards, for example, who served in the Royal Welch Fusiliers, was in a pub, drinking with some of his cronies, old soldiers and Reservists like himself. The usual yarning, or 'line-shooting', as a second generation of Servicemen called it, was going on. One of the company had fought in the Boxer Rising, and by the time he had finished his tale, Richards says, "he had hundreds of Chinks hanging on the gas brackets." Another had been in South Africa, and at the end of his story there wasn't a Boer left. Richards himself had served in India and Burma, and did fearful verbal damage to the Pathans and Dacoits. And then someone rushed into the pub and shouted: "War's broken out. The Sergeant of Police is sticking a notice up now outside the Post Office." So they went out to look at the notice, and that gave them something else to talk about. The Reservists decided that it was too late to report to their depots that night, so they stayed in the pub, still yarning, until what was known, in that Golden Age before the licensing laws, as 'stop tap'. And the next day they went to war.

The B.E.F. of 1914 is always referred to as a 'Regular Army'; so it was, but it is not always realised just what the phrase means. The notion that units simply marched away, pretty well as they existed in their barracks, to active service, is a long way from the truth. In fact it was the Reservists, like Richards and his friends, who made up the greater part of the fighting strength of the Army. The units of the Home Army in peace-time were generally below strength, and full of recent recruits and young soldiers who were only partially trained. All these had to be left behind, and the ranks filled nevertheless. It was for this purpose that the Reserve had been created—this, and reinforcement after battle—so that although the men who went to Mons were Regulars indeed, by no means all of them were physically fully fit at first for the strain of campaigning, nor were they all immediately quite re settled in Army life and methods. In most of the British battalions that fought at Mons the Reservists amounted to fifty per cent of the total strength, in some as much as seventy per cent, while the proportion for the B.E.F. as a whole was sixty per cent. The Continental Armies, having by August just completed the training of the year's batch of conscripts, required comparatively few Reservists to bring them up to strength. When we speak of the marching qualities of the Expeditionary Force, this is worth remembering; for to men out of the habit of marching long distances, and wearing Army boots only just issued to them, the long cobbled roads of northern France under the August sun were torture. Armies may indeed march on their stomachs, but soldiers march on their feet, and these soldiers at times must have regarded their feet as more ferocious enemies than the Germans.

For all at the depots, serving men and Reservists alike, there was plenty to do. On August 5th Commanding Officers were given files of documents—all 'Top Secret'—detailing the exact movements of their units to their un-named ports of embarkation. These were terse orders, crisp and sharp in their precision of detail:

> "Train No. 463Y will arrive at siding B at 12.35 a.m., August 10th.
> You will complete loading by 3.40 a.m.
> This train will leave siding C at 9.45 a.m., August 10th.
> You will march on to the platform at 9.30 a.m. and complete your entraining by 9.40 a.m. . . ."

It was all, some people thought, slightly un-British. It was certainly very efficient. And, above all, it was very secret. Officers came and went on special missions, without a word. The habit of saying as little as possible, and not asking unnecessary questions, was formed quickly. Easily, swiftly, silently, the B.E.F. prepared itself; the atmosphere was serious and professional—though never, this being a British Army, too serious. All the same, the notice: "Officers are particularly requested to pay their mess bills before leaving" was probably serious enough for some. One thing was certain: this Army was too professional for emotional outbursts and wallowings. There was no hatred of Germany, says one of the regimental officers, "but in the true mercenary spirit we would equally readily have fought the French. Our motto was, 'We'll do it. What is it?' " In those days all foreigners were much alike to Englishmen; it had been a different matter, even for 'mercenaries', back in March, when it was a question of coercing Ulster.

Everyone was busy; there was not much time for discussion on the higher level. Nevertheless, some senior officers tried—with varying results—to give their subordinates an idea of what the war would be like. In the 2nd Cavalry Brigade, the Commanding Officer, General de Lisle, took advantage of the fact that one of his officers, Major Bridges,* had been Military Attaché at Brussels. He invited Bridges to address all the officers of the brigade on the subject of the Belgian fortresses which lay in the path of the German advance. Bridges gave an accurate estimate of the holding power of Liège, but, like everyone else, he was deceived by Namur. When the Brigadier asked him how long he thought the war would last, he gave it six months. De Lisle knew better. "Make no mistake, gentlemen," he said, "we are in for a long and bitter war." It was a great piece of good fortune that, in the prevailing atmosphere of optimism and enthusiasm, the new Secretary of State for War, Lord Kitchener, shared this view.

The preparations drew to their conclusion. Lieutenant B. L. Montgomery, of the Royal Warwickshire Regiment, records that it was laid down in the very detailed instructions on mobilisation procedure "that all officers' swords were to go to the armourers' shop on the third day of mobilisation to be sharpened. It was not clear to me why, since I had never used my sword except for saluting. But of course I obeyed the order and my sword was made sharp for war." Lieutenant Montgomery decided that the time had come to obtain advice about the practical side of active service; he asked his C.O. whether it was necessary to take any money with him. The C.O. replied that money was useless, since in war the soldier has everything provided for him. Montgomery nevertheless decided to take ten pounds in gold, and later found it invaluable. He also disregarded another hint from his Commanding Officer, with equal prudence: the C.O. held that it was advisable to go on campaign with short hair, for reasons of hygiene. He caused the regimental barber to remove all his hair with clippers, and looked, says Montgomery, "an amazing sight". He was an amazing man; we shall hear more of him later.

When the trains drew up at their secret destinations, and the troops stepped out of them, the vast majority found themselves at Southampton. This was the embarkation port for personnel; transport and supplies were also sent from Newhaven, Avonmouth and Liverpool.

* Later Lieut.-Gen. Sir Tom Bridges, K.C.B., K.C.M.G., D.S.O., LL.D.

Ample as it was, the complex of docks and sidings at Southampton was fully tested during the five days that covered the main movement of the B.E.F. On one day—the busiest—eighty trains were run into Southampton Docks; an average of thirteen ships was despatched daily—that is, over 50,000 tons gross of shipping per day. During those five days 1,800 special trains were run. There were almost no hitches: the pre-arranged timetable was meticulously kept.

As the transports put out to sea, the masters of the ships were still ignorant of the course they should steer. Sealed orders, only to be opened after departure, contained the names of the French ports where the B.E.F. would be disembarked: Boulogne, Le Havre, Rouen. Advance parties arrived at these places as early as August 7th to prepare the camping grounds and points of assembly for the main bodies following after. At Boulogne, to the delight of the inhabitants, the first detachment to arrive was of Argyll and Sutherland Highlanders, wearing kilts, and marching to the skirl of the bagpipes. They went to work immediately, laying out the camps and lines; and the sites on which they laid them were the very ones where Napoleon's Grand Army had assembled for the invasion of England over a hundred years before—the Marlborough Camp, right beside the great column on the cliffs that commemorates Napoleon's ambition, and the St. Leonard Camp, within sight of the château which had been his headquarters. It was the British Fleet that had brought Napoleon's plans to nothing in 1805, and saved England from invasion; it was the Fleet again that made possible this safe, unobstructed flow of British soldiers into France in 1914, to bring aid against an invasion on a scale beyond all previous experience.

It is frequently the case that the Navy's most effective work is done when it is invisible. The great value of commerce protection, blockade and denying the use of the sea to enemy shipping is easy to understand and to compare with the more obvious but much rarer glamour of battle. What constantly amazes the layman is that so much of this work is apparently done *in absentia*. As the crowded troopships and laden transports crossed and re-crossed the Channel —on the peak day there were 137 passages—the soldiers on board were surprised to find that they saw practically nothing of the Navy. Some smoke on the horizon, an occasional view of a destroyer, dashing past behind a steep bow-wave on its inscrutable mission, and vanishing as swiftly as it appeared—and that was all. It was not the presence of its own ships that told the story of the Navy's power, but the absence of the enemy's. And this absence was secured by the application of the tested methods of naval strategy which had developed over centuries. It is frequently said that the Navy 'convoyed' the B.E.F. across to France. It did no such thing. It was by the strategic location of its squadrons, grouped as striking forces, that the Navy prevented the German Fleet from even attempting to interfere with the Expeditionary Force. The Grand Fleet, based hundreds of miles away to the north, in the Orkneys, contained the main German forces in their harbours; the Channel Fleet, with the Harwich force, and the French Channel flotillas, completely blocked the Channel itself to German light forces. The slim grey shapes which the soldiers had expected to see, perhaps within hailing distance of the transports, were far away, but already teaching the enemy the true meaning of sea-power and of naval tradition.

The main bodies of the B.E.F. began their crossings on August 12th. The 15th, 16th and 17th were the peak days of the movement. A khaki-coloured tide flowed out over the docksides of the ports of disembarkation, into the camps, and out of them again along the roads of the Pas-de-Calais and Picardy towards the first concentration area around Amiens. Everywhere the British Army received a rapturous welcome from the French population. M. Felix Adam, the mayor of Boulogne, issued a poster which set the tone of public reception:

> "My dear Citizens," it ran, "This very day arrive in our town the valiant British troops, who come to co-operate with our brave soldiers to repel the abominable aggression of Germany. . . . Boulogne, which is one of the homes of the Entente Cordiale, will give to the sons of the United Kingdom an enthusiastic and brotherly welcome. The citizens are requested on this occasion to decorate the fronts of their houses with the colours of the two countries."

The citizens gladly complied. The vessels directed on Rouen, steaming up the Seine, found the banks of the river crowded with people waving Union Jacks, most of them home-made, and calling their greetings across the water. The British soldiers roared out their cheers in reply. There were few who did not catch the emotion of the moment—an emotion all the more intense on both sides because it followed, in a wave of relief, the days of uncertainty when no one quite knew what the British Government intended to do. "It was good," says one who was there, "to be an Englishman that day; good to feel that Englishmen then in France could now look Frenchmen squarely in the face."

Of course, there were some contretemps here and there. Even in rapturous Boulogne, the 4th Dragoon Guards, having a boiling hot Sunday to kill, took their horses to the beaches to let men and animals enjoy a cooling bathe—and came out of the water to find themselves looking down the muzzles of two batteries of French '75s, whose teams stood heaving and sweating behind them. An imaginative patriot, out of touch with events, had reported a hostile landing, and the French were taking no risks. Elsewhere serious crises arose when French civil and military authorities, carried away by fervour for the Entente, attempted to kiss senior British officers on both cheeks, frequently in full view of the ranks. It was fortunate that discipline in the B.E.F. of 1914 was so admirable, and morale so high. This was a hazard that had not been legislated for. But there were kisses enough from other quarters that were received with entire enthusiasm. The Army did not have long to enjoy the amenities of the coastal towns, but it was long enough to make a considerable impression, and to cause many an attractive Frenchwoman to wonder whether the legends of British dourness and impassivity had not been somewhat overpainted. Lord Kitchener, percipient in all things, had foreseen something of this. "In this new experience," he told the troops, in a message pasted inside their paybooks, "you may find temptations, both in wine and women. You must entirely resist both temptations, and while treating all women with perfect courtesy you should avoid any intimacy. Do your duty bravely. Fear God. Honour the King." Well, it was not given to all to be able to carry out these lofty precepts to the full. But the B.E.F. did not disgrace itself. That no lasting legacy of bitterness ensued, as the long years of war rolled by, and that so little trouble arose during them, is a tribute to the good sense of Frenchwomen and to the natural decency of the ordinary British soldier.

Through Boulogne flowed all branches of the British Army—mainly infantry at first, still happy with the novelty of their new marching song, *Tipperary*, and with the humour (very 'period' for us) of their endlessly repeated question: "Are we down-hearted? N-o-o-o-o!" and then: "Shall we win? Y-e-e-s-s!" Then came the artillery; Horse Artillery, living up to their tradition as the smartest regiment in the Army; Field Artillery, with their trim, gleaming 18-pounders and howitzers; Heavy Artillery, the long 60-pounders, which were to prove of such inestimable value in the coming battles, drawn by sturdy shire horses. The columns of British artillery moving through the towns of France did much to persuade Frenchmen that we meant business. Then the cavalry arrived, splendidly mounted, but astonishing the French by their habit of walking as much as they rode. It was a practice that was to pay good dividends later. And beside and behind the combat troops came the Royal Engineers, the Service Corps, the Medical Corps, and all the subsidiary units that make up a modern Army.

One small detachment, in unfamiliar uniforms, when it appeared on the quayside at Boulogne, distinguished this Expeditionary Force from all earlier ones, placed it unmistakably in the twentieth century. Dressed in tight, cross-over tunics, wearing their forage caps at a jaunty angle, and their trousers, above leggings and puttees, with a swaggery bulge, smelling slightly of oil, these men were as much an enigma to the British Staff Officers in charge of the disembarkation as to the French civilians who saw them arrive. One Staff Officer, entirely baffled by their strange appearance, and by the vast quantities of weird impedimenta which accompanied them, retired to the telephone.

"I've got some fellows here who call themselves an Aircraft Park," he announced. "What on earth am I supposed to do with them?"

This detachment was, in fact, the mobile base of the young Royal Flying Corps, off to its first campaign. The corps itself had only been in existence for two years, but already it had proved, on manœuvres, to those who were prepared to be convinced, that it was capable of performing notable service. It took the field, in August, 1914, with four squadrons, Nos. 2, 3, 4 and 5 (No. 1 Squadron was the airship squadron), a total of some sixty aircraft. The squadrons flew to France. There is nothing remarkable in that to us now. But it was an historic occasion, for this was the first organised national force to fly to a war overseas. The R.F.C. had come a long way in two years; during the next four its development would be prodigious. The extent of the achievement is summed up in the *Official History of the War In The Air*):

> "By the 1st of November (1910) the Royal Aero Club had issued twenty-two certificates; that is to say, twenty-two pilots, some of them self-taught, and some trained in France, were licensed by the sole British authority as competent to handle a machine in the air. Eight years later, in November, 1918, when the armistice put an end to the active operations of the war, the Royal Air Force was the largest and strongest of the air forces of the world. We were late in beginning, but once we had begun we were not slow."

The four squadrons flew to war in a variety of machines, all of the 'kite-held-together-with-string' type: Blériots, Henri Farmans, Avros, B.E. 8s. The principle of one type for each squadron was not yet accepted, and in any case not yet practicable, in the embryonic condition of the British aircraft industry. However, the diversity of machines, though obviously it increased the problems of the ground crews, did not affect operations. There was no formation flying; each aircraft acted independently in the air. An attempt at collective manœuvre on the way over met with mild disaster. Several aircraft of No. 4 Squadron were damaged by trying to follow their leader down, only to find, too late, that he was making a forced landing in a ploughed field. The first squadron to make the crossing was No. 2 Squadron, on August 13th; the first aircraft left the airfield in England at 6.25 a.m., and the first to arrive at Amiens landed at 8.20 a.m. Their crossing was uneventful. But Lieut. R. M. Vaughan of No. 5 Squadron had an early taste of the discomforts of war. Forced to land near Boulogne on August 15th, he was arrested by the French and held in prison for nearly a week; he was only able to rejoin his squadron on the eve of the Battle of Mons. By this time another un-expected hazard had been encountered: the Flying Corps was in close contact with the B.E.F. "We were rather sorry they had come," remarks Air Marshal Sir Philip Joubert, "because up till that moment we had only been fired on by the French whenever we flew. Now we were fired on by French *and* English. To this day I can remember the roar of musketry that greeted two of our machines as they left the aerodrome and crossed the main Maubeuge-Mons road, along which a British column was proceeding." To minimise this danger, the ground crews, while they were at Maubeuge, painted Union Jacks on the undersides of the wings of each aircraft. But whatever the markings, as pilots of the Second World War will confirm, there is no guaranteed fool-proof method of persuading forces on the ground and sea that aeroplanes are anything but hostile. Fortunately, good shots though many of them were, the British infantry of August, 1914, did not succeed in winging any of our planes. One might, perhaps, anticipate events here with a story of how the infantry had the tables turned on them in an unexpected fashion, after one of these volleys at a passing aircraft. In this case it was, indeed, a German machine, and a whole battalion let fly at it. For once some of the bullets found their target, and the German plane started to come down nearby. The battalion cheered, of course, and their Commanding Officer looked pleased. His expression changed, however, when out of a hedge appeared an old, seedy French Territorial, wiping his rifle through, and looking very smug. "Not a bad shot, eh?" he remarked to the British C.O.

For one man in particular, among the 100,000 soldiers who crossed to France in the first wave of the Expeditionary Force, the moment was singularly and deeply emotional. Field-Marshal Sir John French, the Commander-in-Chief, had passed, in the short space of a few months, from the lowest ebb to the highest peak of his military career. In March, 1914, he held the post which, next to a great command in the field, is the most coveted in the Army—Chief of the Imperial General Staff. But French was not truly a Staff Officer, he was, above all, a "fighting soldier." Originally intended for the Navy, he transferred to the Army when he found that he was not constituted to bear the great heights of the mast-heads at which, in the latter part of the nineteenth century, midshipmen were expected to perform a large part of their training. He became a cavalryman—the most distinguished that Britain has produced since Cromwell. He was one of the few senior officers to come out of the South African War with his reputation enhanced. The operations of his small covering force round Colesberg, which saved the Cape Province from Boer invasion, were long regarded as a model of how such things should be conducted. Later, under Lord Roberts, when the tide turned in our favour, French's dash to Kimberley captured the popular imagination as fully as his Colesberg campaign had won professional esteem. He was marked out for high advancement from that time forward.

Back in England, after the South African War, French graduated to the highest Staff appointment in the Army via the most important peace-time command—Aldershot. Despite his reputation, in the new climate of the reforming Army there were many who doubted whether the qualities that had hitherto distinguished him were the right ones for the task of preparing the spearhead of the future Expeditionary Force for Continental warfare. French may possibly have shared some of these doubts in secret himself. At any rate, a visible change came over him. Lord Esher, the Civil Servant who had probably the deepest insight into Army affairs at that period, said:

> "His mind broadened and his horizon expanded. He displayed qualities of high command, a grasp of tactical problems, and a strategical insight, hitherto unsuspected. It was noticed that a certain aloofness of demeanour grew upon him, although by nature inclined to comradeship. His rides were companionless and his evenings spent in solitary musings . . . he was never free from the haunting obsession of a great war, to which all his powers and faculties were sharpened."

As the omens of war multiplied, French's position seemed ever more secure. He had done a good job at Aldershot; if he was less distinguished at the War Office, at least he was in tune with the work that was being completed there, and his experience added depth to the counsels of the nation. He was fully in accord with the policy of military alliance with France which Wilson was working in top gear to implement. In 1913 he had a personal encounter with German militarism that fully confirmed all his convictions. He had been invited to watch the German cavalry manœuvres of that year, an event in which the Kaiser himself always took an active part. The display was usually on the grand scale, and calculated to leave a very sharp impression on all observers. On this occasion, at the luncheon after the set-piece climax of the whole exciting, disquieting spectacle, the Kaiser turned to French and said: "You have seen how long my sword is; you may find it is just as sharp!" French was a hot-tempered man. The effort of submitting to this bullying flourish must have tried him sorely; its implications remained with him.

Suddenly, in his sixty-second year, with all his faculties of action still intact, all French's work, all the careful tuning, both of himself and of the instrument in his charge, which he had performed over a period of years, seemed to be set at nought. The great Irish crisis of 1914 involved the Home Forces in a predicament as dire as it was unparalleled. Matters came to a head in March, in what is known as the 'Curragh Incident'. The prospect that the Irish Home Rule Bill would shortly become law threw all Ulster into a ferment. Among the Protestants of the north there was fanatical resistance to the idea of being ruled by the Catholic majority of the south. Volunteers were raised and armed, and there was every prospect of Civil War of the bitterest kind. Should this come, obviously the Army would have to intervene. For the ordinary soldiers this task would be disagreeable enough, but for the officers, many of whom came from Northern Ireland, and almost all of whom were privately opposed to the Liberal Government on general principles, despite what it had done for the Army, the prospect was appalling. On March 20th the Commander-in-Chief in Ireland, Sir Arthur Paget, made an alarmist speech to his senior officers which left them with the strong, but false impression that they would shortly be ordered into Ulster to coerce the population into accepting Home Rule. As a result the Adjutant-General at the War Office received the following telegram: "Regret to report brigadier and 57 officers 3rd Cavalry Brigade prefer to accept dismissal if ordered north". In fact, there was no question of this brigade being ordered north; its secret orders would have taken it south in the event of trouble.

Immediately a conflict of interests arose within the Government. For the Cabinet as a whole, the question of military constraint was now raised in reverse in the sharpest manner. It was no longer Ulster, but the Government itself which seemed to be threatened by Army action, and there was a loud demand that the Army should be 'disciplined'. For the Secretary of State for War, Colonel Seely, and for the C.I.G.S., French, there was the dreadful prospect that the Army would disintegrate, just at a time when every well-informed person knew that the peace of Europe was becoming daily more fragile. For Seely and French the most urgent priority was to calm the excited officers down, to correct their wrong impressions, and bring the Army back to its duty. The extent of the cleavage in the Army may be easier to judge, at this distance in time, when we recall that Wilson, holding the post of Director of Military Operations, thought himself fully entitled to impart Government secrets both to the Opposition and to the Ulster Volunteers; and Lord Roberts went so far as to cut French dead in the street, because he thought that the Government's chief military adviser was too sympathetic to it. In the event, Seely and French were able to persuade the cavalry officers to return quietly to their duty; there were no resignations and no dismissals. But the Government appeared to be compromised by a promise that French inserted over his and Seely's signature, to the effect that the Army would not be ordered north. Seely resigned, and French resigned with him. To all intents and purposes his career had come to a full stop at the very moment when he was in expectation of bringing it to its complete fruition. The months that followed were a bitter time. Winston Churchill, who as First Lord of the Admiralty had had close dealings with French before his resignation, saw much of him at this period, and has recorded: "My impression of French, for all his composure, was that he was a heart-broken man."

On August 14th, less than six months later, French and his headquarters crossed the Narrow Seas at the head of the largest, best-equipped and most efficient British Army that had ever left our shores. It was a remarkable reversal of fortune. An emotional man, liable to heights and depths of feeling at any time, beneath his bluff and soldierly exterior, French felt the occasion deeply as he boarded the cruiser *Sentinel* on that dark and somewhat chilly August afternoon to take up his command on foreign soil. His thoughts, as well as his feelings, had plenty to dwell upon. He carried with him Lord Kitchener's instructions, on which he would be required to base all his future conduct. Kitchener breathed a large portion of his far-sighted wisdom into these instructions; but because all was new, and hidden in darkness, their wording was in places necessarily vague and even contradictory. In them lay the germs of controversies that would bedevil the British Command throughout the war.

First, Kitchener laid down French's task:

> "The special motive of the Force under your control is to
> support and co-operate with the French Army . . . in preventing

> or repelling the invasion by Germany of French and Belgian territory and eventually to restore the neutrality of Belgium. . . .
>
> "These are the reasons which have induced His Majesty's Government to declare war, and these reasons constitute the primary objective you have before you."

Then Kitchener continued with a warning:

> "It must be recognised from the outset that the numerical strength of the British Force and its contingent reinforcement is strictly limited, and with this consideration kept steadily in view it will be obvious that the greatest care must be exercised towards a minimum of losses and wastage.
>
> "Therefore, while every effort must be made to coincide most sympathetically with the plans and wishes of our Ally, the gravest consideration will devolve upon you as to participation in forward movements where large bodies of French troops are not engaged and where your Force may be unduly exposed to attack."

And then, quite categorically:

> "In this connection I wish you distinctly to understand that your command is an entirely independent one, and that you will in no case come in any sense under the orders of any Allied General."

Finally:

> "I am sure you fully realise that you can rely with the utmost confidence on the whole-hearted and unswerving support of the Government, of myself, and of your compatriots, in carrying out the high duty which the King has entrusted to you and in maintaining the great tradition of His Majesty's Army."

There was enough in that to think about. To co-operate with the French in preventing or repelling invasion; to restore the neutrality of Belgium; to do this while avoiding heavy losses; nevertheless to 'coincide most sympathetically' with French plans; but to avoid undue exposure on their behalf; to remain at all times independent, although the B.E.F. would amount to only a fraction of the French array, would be operating on French soil, and be entirely dependent on the French for its communications; there were problems here that did not require a genius to perceive them.

As Sir John French landed at Boulogne late that afternoon, and saw the long columns of his Army streaming away to their historic camping-grounds in the setting rays of a belated sun, he had a moment of sadness, reflecting on how many of them would never see

England again, but mainly his mood, like that of his Staff, was joyful and optimistic. The day for which they had all prepared had come; they did not doubt their abilities to measure up to it; they did not know what hazards fate had prepared for them.

2

Meetings

WHEN THE ARMY LEFT the disembarkation ports, and headed off down the cobbled, poplar-lined roads of northern France, through the dusty towns and straggling villages and over the rolling downlands of Picardy, its first point of concentration was Amiens, and then the region beside the fortress of Maubeuge, close to the Belgian frontier, due south of Mons. This was the concentration area selected long before, the one marked on Henry Wilson's little section of sacred map at Mars-la-Tour; it brought the British Army to the extreme left flank of the French, a logical place for it, and one where the only danger seemed to be that it might miss a lot of the fun when the great French offensive began. Yet although this area had been selected a long time before, the B.E.F.'s march towards it had by no means followed automatically.

The unofficial military agreement with France had always presupposed simultaneous mobilisation in both countries. The extreme deliberation with which the British Government entered the war made this impossible. France and Germany both ordered full mobilisation on August 1st (though we now know that Germany had already taken many of the first steps of mobilisation without any formal public announcement); on August 3rd Germany declared war on France, but it was not until the following day that the British ultimatum to Germany expired, and mobilisation was ordered in the United Kingdom. The Entente therefore commenced operations at a disadvantage—suffering from a delay which not only produced the gravest mistrust of British intentions in France, but perturbed and enraged the planners at the War Office, Henry Wilson above all. He now held the post of Sub-Chief of the General Staff of the B.E.F., under Lieut.-General Sir Archibald Murray. Murray was a con-

scientious and reliable soldier, but French, while he was prepared
leave great responsibility and a huge volume of work to Murray,
leaned much more on Wilson for ideas. All three of them, together
with the commanders of the I and II Army Corps of the B.E.F., Sir
Douglas Haig and Sir James Grierson, had been summoned by the
Prime Minister, Mr. Asquith, to the War Council at 10 Downing
Street at 4 p.m. on August 5th. It was only at this historic meeting
that, after lengthy discussion, the decisions were taken which confirmed the long-standing plans of the Operations Department: that
the B.E.F. should go to Maubeuge, as arranged, and that it should
consist of the six infantry divisions and one large cavalry division
that Lord Haldane had always intended. The members of this
august assembly were not yet aware of what the Government had let
itself in for, in bringing Lord Kitchener into its ranks; it was not long
before they learned.

Earl Kitchener of Khartoum took up his duties as Secretary of
State for War on August 5th, and immediately hurled into the work
of his office the whole range of his dynamic powers of creation and
destruction. He was able to discern at once, through those processes
of personal intuition on which he had depended all his life, what few
soldiers and even fewer politicians fully perceived, that the war
would be a long one, and that Britain must expand her Army
enormously in order to wage it. This expansion of the Army became
his first and most compelling task. "Even if Lord Kitchener had
done nothing more than this," remarked one of his severest critics,
Lord Esher, "his taking office would have been an inestimable
service to the country. . . ." For a long time he was referred to as a
supreme organiser, because of this achievement; but this was not so.
One of his best friends, Ian Hamilton, wrote: ". . . he hated
organisations; he smashed organisations. . . . He was a Master of Expedients." And this would seem to be the truth. For Lord Kitchener,
contrary to popular belief, was not a military 'expert'; he was not a
qualified Staff Officer; he did not even properly understand the
functions of a Staff. He was, however, a leader, in the sense of filling
all those who served under him with deep confidence, through his
brilliant intuition, his unrivalled capacity for improvisation and his
immense force of character.

The whole of Kitchener's career in the Army until 1914 had been spent overseas, in Egypt, South Africa and India; he returned with more than a touch of the oriental despot in his manners and his methods. Everything that he did was a personal endeavour; he scarcely knew how to delegate. This defect had always been noticeable in him. In the Sudan, in 1898, General Rawlinson, then an officer on Kitchener's tiny staff, had written: "The one serious criticism that I have is that this is too much a one-man show." Drawing on his huge reserves of mental and physical energy, Kitchener made everything he touched a one-man show. It worked in the Sudan; it worked (more or less) in South Africa; it certainly set things moving in the congealed conditions of India in the first decade of the century. But, applied to the overwhelming problems of modern war in Europe in 1914, it would not do. However, it has to be admitted that he was working under a handicap for which he was not responsible; it arose out of the false estimate of the War which was then current in the Army and in the Government. Believing that the War could not last long, and that while it lasted the only important place to be was with the B.E.F., almost all the Departmental Heads and senior Staff Officers had been absorbed into French's G.H.Q. Kitchener, says Lord Esher, "glanced round the War Office for help, but could find none. Whitehall had been swept clean of soldiers of experience and talent. They had been gathered into the Expeditionary Force overseas, and with the exception of Sir John Cowans, the Q.M.G., he found aged and tired men who trembled before him and his reputation." Disastrous in itself, this virtual abolition of what should have been the Army's brain- and nerve-centre at the very outset of the war immediately produced the most serious consequences.

Above all, it was Kitchener's sheer lack of knowledge of European armies and military organisation that was to have the worst results and it was here that an adequate Staff could have corrected and aided him. Intuition told him what needed to be done; all his practical experience tended to draw him into wrong methods of doing it. The raising of the New Armies—his greatest achievement— is the most complete example of this. He entirely set aside the Territorial system which Lord Haldane had envisaged as the natural manner of expanding the Army, through the County Associations. "The result," says Haldane, "was the confusion which arises from sudden departure from settled principles." The reason for Kitchener's rejection of the Territorial system is interesting. Having taken part in the Franco-Prussian War of 1870 on the French side, he had grimly vivid memories of the bad performances of the French Territorial troops of those days. He entirely ignored the fact that the British Territorials of 1914, enthusiastic, mainly young, volunteer citizen-soldiers, were utterly different from the old French reservists who shared their title. Such is the power of a word, and such is the cost of the personal method.

In the higher direction of the War, also, Kitchener was ignorant of the details and reasoning of existing plans. Partly because of this, and also partly because of his mistrust of the Territorial Force, on which it had always been agreed that the responsibility of Home Defence would rest (behind the shield of the Navy), among his first acts was the reversal of one of the two decisions taken at the Great War Council on August 5th. He decided that it would be unsafe to send all six Regular divisions abroad at once, and so the Expeditionary Force that French led to Mons consisted of only two Corps, not three—four infantry divisions and five brigades of cavalry. There was plenty of heart-burning over this, and in the light of what we now know about the impotence of the German Navy, the decision seems wrong. Nevertheless it can be argued that the absence of the two extra divisions at Mons was providential. We shall see how, in the confused mental climate of Allied Headquarters, the dangers of over-confidence were very real. More strength on the ground might have made them fatal.

Having already set aside one decision of the War Council, Kitchener found himself growing increasingly uneasy about the other. The more he brooded upon the campaign into which the B.E.F. was blithely marching, the greater this uneasiness grew. The quality was at work in him which stood him in the best stead—that apparently baseless intuition which practically never erred. He was not as yet able to advance conclusive arguments to support his fears, he had no statistics to present to those who disagreed; but with each day that passed the conviction solidified within him that the Germans were about to attempt one of their much-advertised enveloping manœuvres on a scale that nobody had so far conceived. He felt more and more certain that the B.E.F. might easily advance into a gigantic trap. On

August 12th, two days before French and his Staff set off for France, Colonel Repington, *The Times* military correspondent, brought off a remarkable journalistic coup: he was able to produce a map "showing the concentration of the German Armies on the French frontier, giving the position of every Army Corps. . . . and I think with fair exactitude. . . . This map completely exposed the German aim of enveloping the French left by a march through Belgium, and had the proper conclusions been drawn by the French Staff from the indications on which the map was based, the great misfortunes of the opening of the war would have been avoided." It may have been the sight of this map in *The Times* that morning that brought Kitchener's anxiety to a head; Repington's reputation, like that of his newspaper, was not lightly to be set aside. At any rate, that afternoon Kitchener saw French, with Murray, Wilson and three officers of the French Military Mission.

It was an irritating interview for Wilson. They assembled at the War Office at three o'clock, and there, says Wilson, "we wrangled with K. for three hours. K. wanted (the B.E.F.) to go to Amiens, and he was incapable of understanding the delays and difficulties of making such a change, nor the cowardice of it, nor the fact that either in French victory or defeat we would be equally useless. He still thinks the Germans are coming north of the Meuse in great force, and will swamp us before we concentrate." It is an ironic reflection that already, while this little group of British and French officers were heatedly arguing, six against one, the Germans were completing their preparations for that very advance across the Meuse which Kitchener had predicted. "There is no longer question," says Wilson's biographer, "but that Lord Kitchener formed a far more correct opinion of the situation as between the Entente and the Central Powers as a whole, than did Wilson or, apparently, anybody else on the staff of G.H.Q." Nevertheless, on this occasion it was Kitchener who gave way, and the B.E.F. was permitted to continue its march to Maubeuge.

G.H.Q. crossed to France on August 14th; on the 16th the main landings of the B.E.F. were completed; by the 20th it was fully assembled in the Maubeuge area. The interval had been a busy time for Sir John French. On the day after his arrival he went to Paris to

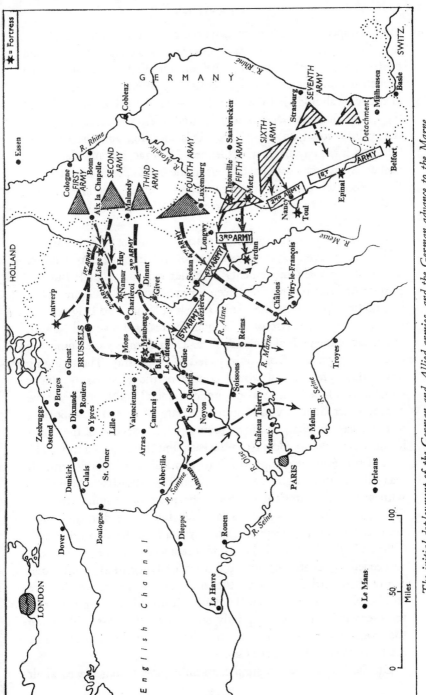

The initial deployment of the German and Allied armies, and the German advance to the Marne

pay his respects to the French Government and meet the Minister of war, M. Messimy. French was impressed by the cheerful optimism of the President, M. Poincaré, who told him that the attitude of the French nation was calm and determined. It was arranged that the next day he should visit the Commander-in-Chief, General Joffre, at the Grand Quartier Général, then located at Vitry-le-François, a tiny, sleepy little town on the Marne. This meeting, and the one that followed it the day after, with General Lanrezac, commander of the French Army immediately adjacent to the B.E.F., were both crucial. But before we consider what happened at these meetings, it will perhaps be best to review the course of the War itself, now just under a fortnight old.

Great modern armies cannot be assembled and let loose in a matter of hours, nor even days; it was not until well into the third week of war that the main movements of either side developed. But important preliminary steps had been taken at once. The Germans had lost no time in pushing the heads of their columns into Belgium and advancing upon the two great Belgian fortresses, Liège and Namur, which lay in the path of their advance. Their Armies were numbered from 1 to 7, reading from right to left of their array. The swinging tip of their great wheel would consist of the First Army, under General von Kluck, the Second, under General von Bülow, and the Third, under General von Hausen. The largest, and most important of these was the First, on the extreme right, but several of the Corps in this Army had to come from the east, and this required time. The task of preparing its progress fell to von Bülow's Second Army. It was this Army that attacked Liège, making a disastrous beginning with a headlong attempt to storm the place on August 5th. The Germans suffered heavy losses, and fell into great disorder. They were rallied by the Deputy Chief of Staff of the Second Army, Colonel Ludendorff. He led them to a renewed assault next day, and succeeded in penetrating into the town of Liège itself; the Second Army then settled down to the siege of the forts, which were stubbornly defended by the Belgians. Meanwhile the remainder of the German Armies were quietly completing their assembly along the frontier, awaiting the moment when the whole mass would be ready to execute its modern Cannae.

On the French side, a similar assembly was taking place. Their

Armies, also, numbered from right to left, the 1st Army being in Alsace, and the 5th on the northern flank, with its headquarters at Rethel, facing the Ardennes. On August 6th, when Ludendorff was pushing into Liège, the French sent their Cavalry Corps, under its dapper, hard-working, loyal little General, Sordet, northwards into Belgium. The next day, at the other extremity of their line, they struck somewhat south of eastwards into Alsace with a detachment of their 1st Army. All their attention was focused upon the frontier with Germany, and this was a preliminary manœuvre designed to secure the flank of their great advance into Lorraine. It was also designed to hearten French public opinion. Unfortunately, the Germans reacted violently to this French move, and soon drove them back across the frontier. By the 11th a slight dent was perceptible in the over-riding optimism of G.Q.G., General Lanrezac, commanding the 5th Army, although not yet ready to abjure the settled doctrine of the French strategists, was receiving information that made him increasingly uneasy about his left flank. He obtained permission to move one of his Army Corps northward to Givet on the banks of the Meuse. This occurred, it will be noted, on the day *before* Kitchener had to defend his anxiety about this very area against the representatives of both British and French Headquarters.

On August 12th the writing appeared on the wall for the gallant defenders of Liège; the Germans brought into position their giant 42-cm. siege artillery, and began to subject the forts to a merciless pounding. On the same day, however, the Belgians fought a successful delaying rearguard action at Haelen against the leading cavalry of von Kluck's Army. The Austrians, on this day, began their first advance into Serbia; it was this quarrel that had brought the War about, but their doings had already been relegated to a significance that was scarcely even secondary. The Western Front assumed immediately the dominating role that it retained throughout the War. And here the German plans were now unfolding. In conformity with von Schlieffen's original idea, from which he had not yet brought himself to depart, von Moltke ordered his Sixth and Seventh Armies in Lorraine and Alsace to yield to French pressure. Accordingly, on the 14th, when the French resumed their advance in that quarter, they found themselves able to make encouraging progress. It may have been this progress that caused Joffre to express himself very buoyantly to Lanrezac, who came to see him that day to mention his increasing anxiety about the left wing. Lanrezac returned to his headquarters apparently convinced by what Joffre told him, and the general mood at G.Q.G. was highly optimistic. Lanrezac, however, found plenty to make him change his mind when he returned to Rethel. On the 15th, the day that Sir John French was in Paris, German cavalry appeared on the Meuse at Dinant. The possibility of a blow from that direction had seriously to be reckoned with. Lanrezac made new representations to Joffre, and received permission to assemble his Army in a new position, not opposite the Ardennes, but between the Meuse and the Sambre, on a line from Givet to Maubeuge, thus linking directly with the B.E.F. It was on this day that Joffre issued his *Instruction Particulière* No. 10, which first admitted that the main German effort was likely to be on the right wing; a supplement to the *Instruction*, issued the following day, ordered the French 4th Army, on the right of the 5th, to organise a defensive position while awaiting the order to advance. This was the first hint of anything but the most offensive spirit in French orders, the first suggestion that they might not retain the initiative. Against this background of events, the commander of the British Expeditionary Force went to meet the French generals who would most closely affect its destiny.

General Joseph Jacques Césaire Joffre was the same age as French, sixty-two. He was an officer of Engineers who, since he had taken part in the defence of Paris as a subaltern in 1870-71, had risen to the top of the French Army by easy stages, without any remarkable display of brilliance on the way. Before the War broke out he held the post of Chief-of-Staff, a position into which he had been levered as the nominee of the offensive school of strategists, not because of any particularly forceful ideas of his own, but because he was a relatively uncontroversial, reassuring figure who could be depended on to pacify the politicians. It is hard to think of anyone less like the traditional concept of the French General Officer. Immensely tall and burly, he towered over the squat figure of Sir John French as he did over most of his own subordinates. His manner was placid and phlegmatic to a degree. "He was," says General Sir Edward Spears, who, in his role of liaison officer, saw much of Joffre at this time, "impenetrably calm. Very often this trait

44

baffled his subordinates. At times when expected to speak he did not utter a word. He has been known to arrive at a headquarters, listen in silence to what was said, and step back into his car without opening his mouth, leaving queries, questions and requests for orders buzzing unvoiced in the heads of those he left behind." As a witness of some such scenes, Spears remarked that they had their comic aspect. "The group of generals and Staff Officers would remain riveted to the ground, gazing in dismay at the fast disappearing motor. When Joffre had finally vanished in a cloud of dust they would look at each other with consternation, turn their hands out in the expressive French gesture that means 'What will you?' and shrugging their shoulders re-enter the headquarters building."

Partly because of these characteristics, and partly also because he was identified with a disastrous school of strategic thought, Joffre came to be regarded by many later as a stupid man. He was dismissed after the failures of 1916, and though given the rank of Marshal of France in recognition of his earlier services, his reputation has remained largely under a cloud ever since. Yet there were always many who regretted his going, particularly in the British Army. His dourness and his silence were not qualities likely to distress British soldiers; when combined with the almost invariable courtesy and reliability which characterised his relations with the British Command, they added up to a very good impression which survived the tribulations of the Alliance almost intact. Certainly his first impact on Sir John French was a favourable one. "He struck me at once," says French, "as a man of strong will and determination, very courteous and considerate, but firm and steadfast of mind and purpose, and not easily turned or persuaded. He appeared to me to be capable of exercising a powerful influence over the troops he commanded and as likely to enjoy their confidence." These first impressions were most important, and it is notable that even after the War French was prepared to affirm that "everything I then thought of General Joffre was far more than confirmed throughout the year and a half of fierce struggle during which I was associated with him. . . . History will rank him as one of the supremely great leaders". Well, History has not done so; but History would be less than just if it failed to notice the qualities of steadfastness, patience and iron courage that lay under Joffre's flat tones and unemphatic manner.

Among his own generals, whatever may have been his intellectual failings, his personality dominated; he maintained an absolute discipline in the higher ranks of the French Army, and during the weeks that were to come this discipline was tested to the full. Joffre's authority never wavered; his stature grew in defeat.

At the head of Joffre's Staff stood the more vivacious figure of General Belin, and below him the vast, seventeen-stone bulk of General Berthelot. Sir John French was almost as pleased with them as he was with their Chief. He was struck, as everyone was, who ever came in contact with it, by the atmosphere of G.Q.G. "There was a complete absence of fuss, and a calm, deliberate confidence was manifest everywhere." French, for his part, made an equally good impression on Joffre: "He gave me at once the feeling that he was a loyal comrade-in-arms, firmly attached to his own ideas and, while bringing us his full support, anxious not to compromise his Army in any way." Joffre's reaction to French's independent command was characteristic. "I perfectly well understood this point; it was entirely natural that England should not consent to subordinate her troops to any Allied commander. I never had any illusions on this subject, although I realised that the absence of a single authority to direct all the Allied forces composing our left would be a serious cause of weakness." Joffre was too big a man to fret about something that could not be altered; he preferred to "try to get the best results out of collaboration and mutual confidence".

At their meeting, Joffre conveyed a strong impression of his offensive intentions to French, and recommended to him his future neighbour, General Lanrezac. This officer was in high esteem at G.Q.G. at this period; Spears, who was liaison officer between Lanrezac's Army and the B.E.F., records: "He was the star turn . . . all at G.Q.G. had been impressed by his determination, and by his declarations in favour of early offensive action." Joffre's A.D.C. told Spears that "the British Army would have to hurry up if they were going to see any of the fun, since General Lanrezac was not going to delay for slow-coaches. . . ." French was to encounter this "veritable lion" the next day. We have seen that underneath his aggressive exterior Lanrezac was already beginning to have doubts; these were growing upon him with every hour that passed. It was somewhat unfortunate that Sir John's visit to Joffre coincided with the last stages of extreme cordiality between G.Q.G. and the Commander of the 5th Army.

While French and Joffre were meeting, great events were beginning to unfold on the battle-fronts. The last of the Liège forts fell on that day, blown to pieces by the great shells of the Austrian howitzers which the German Army had brought up against them. On the Eastern Front, the Austrians themselves were continuing their advance into Serbia, and the Russians were commencing theirs towards East Prussia. The French were still carrying out manœuvres strangely at variance with each other: advancing eastwards in Lorraine and Alsace, but elsewhere performing a "general taking ground to the left", i.e. northwards. This was particularly the case with their 5th Army, and also with their 4th, while on this day the 3rd Army formed a detachment called the Army of Lorraine, whose duty was to mask the great German fortress of Metz. The B.E.F. was completing its disembarkation. At sea, the Navy's command of the oceanic trade routes was complete, and its ascendancy over the enemy fleet fully established.

August 17th was the day on which Sir John French first experienced acutely the difficulties of High Command. In the morning he went to Rethel to meet General Lanrezac, of whom he had heard such glowing accounts at G.Q.G. It was a most unfortunate meeting, but an excellent illustration of the significance of personality in war. General Lanrezac, it must be admitted, remains to this day one of the outstanding enigmas of the First World War. His tenure of command of the 5th Army was a brief one, and terminated his active military career; to some people, in consequence, he has appeared as a victim sacrificed by the wrong-headed clique that was then in charge of the French Army. Others have set him down simply as a failure, one of many who, when the moment of stress came, could not live up to the high reputations that they had won in peace-time, at Staff lectures and exercises. French, for example, later summed him up as "the most complete example, amongst the many this war has afforded, of the Staff College 'pedant', whose 'superior education' had given him little idea of how to conduct war". But French had reason to dislike him, as we shall now see.

Like Joffre, Lanrezac was a big man; but his height and size did not convey Joffre's impression of solidity and strength. Spears took good note of him on joining the headquarters of the 5th Army; at their first meeting Lanrezac was leaning on the balustrade of the flight of steps leading into the old house, in the pretty, sloping square of Rethel, where the Army Headquarters had been set up. "The Army Commander," says Spears, "was a big flabby man with an emphatic corporation. His moustache had more grey than white in it, as had his hair. His face was weather-beaten and dark, and his cheeks and lower lip hung rather loosely. He was looking upward, his head tilted forward, and appeared to be in a bad temper . . . I was struck by the fact that his eyeglasses were hitched over his right ear, a trick he much favoured." Beside Lanrezac stood his Chief-of-Staff, General Hély d'Oissel, a tall, slim, smart, somewhat aloof officer whose good manners were often in sharp contrast with those of his superior.

Once again Sir John French was dwarfed by his ally. And this time a feature of the war came into play which was to last throughout its course, and bring about endless friction and misunderstanding; almost no senior French officer could speak English, and very few British could manage anything more than schoolboy French. When there was goodwill and consideration, as between Joffre and French, this did not greatly matter, given competent interpreters. But when these attitudes were absent it was another story. And there was no doubt that they were lacking on this occasion. Colonel Huguet, Head of the French Mission at G.H.Q., an officer who did not go out of his way, when compiling his Memoirs, to favour the British, has recorded with amazement the first words addressed to him by Hély d'Oissel as French and his Staff were arriving: "Well, here you are (meaning the B.E.F.)—it is just about time. If we are beaten it will be thanks to you." The state of mind indicated by this astonishing remark, says Spears, explains many of the misunderstandings that were to follow. The remark itself, he adds, "can only be explained by the fact that the commander of the 5th Army was already 'rattled'". But there was worse to follow.

It appears fairly certain that French and Lanrezac retired together for a short time, without benefit of the presence of any Staff Officer or interpreter. What they can have communicated to each other, beyond irritation, it is impossible to imagine. Indeed, among the officers awaiting their pleasure outside, somewhat feeble jokes were being made on the lines of: "I bet they are asking each other what has become of the penknife belonging to the gardener's uncle." At any rate, they were not long together, and when they returned Lanrezac quickly showed that he was out of temper. Spears records the story of what then ensued, told to him by a British officer who witnessed it: "Sir John, stepping up to a map in the 3ème (Operations) Bureau, took out his glasses, located a place with his finger, and said to Lanrezac: 'Mon Général, est-ce-que. . . .?' His French then gave out, and turning to one of his staff, he asked: 'How do you say 'to cross the river' in French?' He was told, and proceeded: 'Est-ce-que les Allemands vont traverser la Meuse à— à——?' Then he fumbled over the pronunciation of the name. 'Huy' was the place, unfortunately one of the most difficult words imaginable to pronounce, the 'u' having practically to be whistled. It was quite beyond Sir John. 'Hoy' he said at last, triumphantly. 'What does he say? What does he say?' exclaimed Lanrezac. Somebody explained that the Marshal wanted to know whether in his opinion the Germans were going to cross the river at Huy? Lanrezac shrugged his shoulders impatiently. 'Tell the Marshal,' he said curtly, 'that in my opinion the Germans have merely gone to the Meuse to fish.' "

Shortly after this, the meeting came to an end. It had been disastrous. Lanrezac, undoubtedly worried (and with good reason, as we shall see), self-assertive and dogmatic by nature, had evidently formed the impression that French was an ass, as well as being an Englishman, which was already bad enough. Like many other officers of the French offensive school, Lanrezac was disposed to consider that the only soldiers fit for modern war were the French and German active divisions. All else, Reserve divisions, Territorials, etc., he was inclined to class as rabble; from now onwards he seemed to lump in the British Army with this category. He could not have made a worse mistake, but he took no steps to test out his opinion or correct it. In fact, he only saw French once more, and then at Joffre's behest, and under his eye. French, for his part, although his ignorance of the language concealed the full quality of the slight from him, was perfectly well aware from Lanrezac's manner that he had been treated rudely. A deep distrust of Lanrezac was planted in him. "I left General Lanrezac's Headquarters," he says, "believing that the Commander-in-Chief had over-rated his ability." But in one respect he came away quite certain in his mind: that Lanrezac had no other idea than to attack the enemy as soon as possible.

In conveying this impression so strongly, Lanrezac had been less than frank. For it was on this day that the Germans completed their concentration and began to set their main bodies in motion. The Intelligence Bureau of the French 5th Army began to receive ominous information, indicating for the first time that the weight of the German right wing might be seriously larger than the French had supposed. There were indications, also, of what its intentions might be. The German forces reported at Huy, the place whose name had so thoroughly defeated Sir John French, were drawn from the German Second Army. Their movements had been tracked by Lanrezac's Intelligence officers with some accuracy for several days. At Huy, they would be crossing the River Meuse from south to north, that is, in a direction *away* from France, into Belgium. The only reason why they should do this would be in conformity with a wide flanking movement which could only spell grave peril to the left wing of the 5th Army—and the B.E.F. In other words, French's question had been very much to the point, no matter how badly expressed, and Lanrezac's answer not only rude, but grossly inadequate. He himself was quite aware of these possible implications. Reporting to Joffre that night, Lanrezac said: "As the area of detrainment of the British Army is very close to the Sambre, the 5th Army, which *in the event of a retirement** would not have at its disposal enough roads, would be obliged to make incursions into the British area." He suggested that the possibility of the B.E.F. concentrating further back should be studied. "In the event of a retirement . . ." French had carried away with him the conviction that they had "arrived at a mutual understanding which included no idea or thought of 'retreat'". Joffre still regarded Lanrezac as a devoted apostle of the offensive. And yet the idea of retreat was already in his mind, before his Army had even completed its concentration. Events were to show that the idea itself had vastly more validity than the theories of G.Q.G., which were currently being accepted without question by G.H.Q. But it is indicative of a disturbing defect in Lanrezac's character that he should continue—and

* Author's italics.

it must have been quite deliberate—to conceal from both his Chief and his Ally the main-springs of his conduct. It may be argued that no one would have listened to him, if he had expressed his true fears. Granted the over-heated optimism of G.Q.G., that is probably true. But would that have been worse than the risk of complete misunderstanding which he chose to run, with the certainty added to it, had he cared to face it, that no matter how right he might prove to be, confidence in him personally would come to an end the moment the deception was revealed? We can see now, at this distance in time, that Lanrezac was trapped by the delusions which obsessed the French High Command. One sympathises with him. But it is impossible not to regard some of his struggles and wriggles in the snares of these delusions as undignified and squalid.

All this, of course, was hidden from French on that day. His own headquarters was in the process of being set up at Le Cateau, and when he returned there from Rethel he was greeted with sad and disconcerting news. Sir James Grierson, the commander of his II Corps, had died suddenly in the train on the way to his own H.Q. Grierson was widely regarded as one of the cleverest (in the best sense) and most capable officers in the British Army. Unlike the majority, he was a good linguist. He had served as Military Attaché in Berlin, where, as well as learning to speak fluent German, he had acquired a deep knowledge of the German Army. He also spoke French excellently, and astonished French officers with his knowledge of French military history. He was a man of humour and vision, well read, and much liked throughout the Army. It must also be stated that he had other claims to fame. General Bridges refers to him as a "bon viveur who could hold his own in any company. The most bemedalled officer in the Army, he would jokingly admit that the collection on his ample chest commemorated many a hard-fought battle with the knife and fork". It would seem that those battles had taken a worse toll of him than he knew.

Apart from the question of personal friendship, French felt the loss of Grierson as a calamity to the Army. It was to bring difficulties to him which he could not foresee. He immediately asked Kitchener to send him, as a replacement, Sir Herbert Plumer, who later became the distinguished commander of the British Second Army. But Kitchener, without further reference to French, sent out General Sir

Horace Smith-Dorrien. Whether the discords that were later to arise between French and Smith-Dorrien would have occurred anyway, or whether their relationship might have been warmer had Kitchener been less arbitrary,* is hard to say. French perceived slights easily, whether they were intended or not, and in a matter of this importance was justified in feeling that his views counted and should have been respected.

Grierson was a close personal friend of Haig, who undoubtedly felt the loss deeply, as French did. It is possible that had Grierson lived, not only would relations between G.H.Q. and II Corps have been better, but relations between the two Army Corps themselves. Certainly, after his death, co-operation between them left much to be desired. Nor was there any promise of good understanding between I Corps Headquarters and G.H.Q. On the previous day General Charteris, one of Haig's Staff Officers, and also a close friend, noted in his diary:

> " D. H. unburdened himself today. He is greatly concerned about the composition of British G.H.Q. He thinks French quite unfit for high command in time of crisis. . . . He says French's military ideas are not sound; that he has never studied war; that he is obstinate, and will not keep with him men who point out even obvious errors. He gives him credit for good tactical powers, great courage and determination. . . ."

These were strong views, to be uttered even before the campaign had opened. It was an ominous beginning.

---

* NOTE: Kitchener had misgivings, but suppressed them.

3

The Fog of War

THE FOUR DAYS that followed French's visit to Lanrezac were dark days for the Allied High Command, dark with ignorance and misconception. Most of this stemmed from G.Q.G., where facts were commencing a struggle against preconceived ideas that would prove to be as arduous as the actual fight against the enemy. And in these early days, with Wilson as their advocate, French ideas reigned supreme at G.H.Q.; the British Intelligence Department was to prove itself equal to the French very shortly—Joffre himself acknowledged the debt he owed to information from British sources, mainly the young Royal Flying Corps—but at this stage British Intelligence could scarcely win a hearing if it differed at all significantly from the dicta of G.Q.G.

On the day after his journey to Rethel, when French held his first conference of Corps commanders at Le Cateau, he informed them that a substantial body of German troops was being pushed across the Meuse in a northern and western direction. "It is confidently believed," said the French bulletin, "that at least five Army Corps and two or three cavalry divisions will move against the French frontiers south-west, on a great line between Brussels and Givet." Henry Wilson, noting this information in a letter to his wife that day, displayed his astonishing intellectual resilience with the remark: "The Germans appear to be massing more and more troops up on the north side (of the Meuse), so after all, our prophecies look as though they were going to come true." He had already forgotten, apparently, that it was just this prophecy that he had "wrangled with Kitchener" against, only six days before, in London. But in any case, neither Wilson nor any other Allied Staff Officer yet realised the true significance of the development of the German right wing implied in this appreciation.

The strain of attempting to twist facts to fit theories is clearly visible in the Instruction issued by Joffre, dated 8 a.m. August 18th, embodying all this information. It accepted that the German right wing might comprise as many as fifteen Army Corps, operating in two groups. It was the northern group whose activities would affect the French 5th Army and the B.E.F. Joffre's conclusion, inspired, no doubt, by Plan XVII, was that: "The enemy may engage only a fraction of his right wing group north of the Meuse. While his centre is engaged frontally by our 3rd and 4th Armies, the other part of his northern group, south of the Meuse, may seek to attack the left flank of our 4th Army." In other words, he discounted a wide wheel by the Germans and remained full enough of optimism to see in the enemy's known movements an excellent opportunity for out-flanking them with his own offensive. In this contingency, Lanrezac would attack the flank of the Germans menacing the 4th Army, leaving to the British and Belgians the "task of dealing with the German forces to the north of the Meuse and of the Sambre"—as though these were only a covering detachment, whose destruction would be a secondary task.

Naturally, in this frame of mind, he found Lanrezac's gloomy prognostication of retirement very distasteful. His reply was sharp: "There must be no question of doing anything but holding the present positions." This, coupled with the Instruction, produced its effect on Lanrezac; reporting the concentration of his Army, he told Joffre that by the 20th he would be able to counter-attack any German force which attempted to get at the left flank of the neigh-bouring 4th Army by an advance between Namur and Charleroi, "and to throw them back into the Sambre". Even, he said, if his leading corps should be attacked before the others were up, and forced temporarily to retire, as soon as it received support "it would resume, together with them, the offensive between the Sambre and the Meuse". Altogether a very fiery and aggressive document; Joffre concluded that Lanrezac's deviations were done with. Neverthe-less, they had disturbed him; his confidence in the commander of the 5th Army was never quite the same again.

Behind the veil that lay between the opposing Armies, the remorse-less facts of the German advance were very different from the happy surmises of G.Q.G. It was not fifteen German Army Corps that the left wing of the Allies would have to contend with, but twenty-eight: the First, Second, Third, Fourth and Fifth Armies. And the northern group of these, the swinging loop, comprising the First, Second and Third Armies, contained sixteen Corps, with six extra Landwehr brigades and five cavalry divisions, almost the full weight of which would fall upon the four corps and three Reserve divisions of the 5th Army and the two Corps of the B.E.F., with four cavalry divisions between them. Granted that aerial reconnaissance was in its infancy, granted the habitual fog of war, the extent of the error in French calculations stands as an everlasting reminder of the folly of preconceptions that take no account of the enemy. The first von Moltke once remarked at a Staff exercise: "Gentlemen, I have observed that there are always three courses open to the enemy, and that he usually takes the fourth." A little cogitation in this spirit would have saved the French much grief; fortunately for the B.E.F. there was at least one highly-placed officer at G.H.Q. who was shrewd enough to take disagreeable possibilities into account. The Quartermaster-General, Sir William Robertson, recognised that, "it was my business to be prepared for the worst that might happen as well as for the best. He is merely a fool who, holding a high position in war, refuses to contemplate anything but success." This realisation was to serve the Army well; but for the time being all was optimism, and nothing was dreamt of but success.

It was on August 19th that the Royal Flying Corps carried out the first aerial reconnaissance on active service in its history. Two machines, a Blériot and a B.E., went up at 9.30 a.m., without observers, to see what they could see. The Blériot was piloted by Captain P. B. Joubert de la Ferté, now better known as Air Chief Marshal Sir Philip Joubert. His companion, Lieutenant Mapplebeck, was to go north; Joubert was ordered to inspect the country west of Brussels and report on any evidence of enemy troops. The weather was somewhat cloudy, and what with this and general unfamiliarity with the region, as well as the difficulty of using a one-to-a-million map, both pilots very quickly lost themselves. This was by no means an unusual experience in those days. It was considered rather bad form actually to come down and ask people the way, but under ordinary conditions all airmen were prepared to have to do this. On this occasion, however, there was the grave risk of finding oneself in enemy hands; both pilots were acutely aware of it. "I wandered round Western Belgium for some time," says Joubert, "and then seeing a large town over which the Belgian flag seemed still to be flying, I landed on the parade ground. I discovered that this was Tournai, still in Belgian hands, and I was given a most excellent lunch by the commandant of the garrison. Leaving an hour later, I lost myself again very quickly. Finally I recognised the Bruges Ship Canal, flew south from there, and landed near Courtrai. Here my reception was not at all cordial. The local police threatened to put me in jail. I was saved by the kindness of a little North of Ireland linen manufacturer, who was visiting Courtrai, where there are a lot of spinning mills. He placed a Union Jack on my aircraft, and the tone immediately improved. I got what I wanted, which was petrol, and the directions how to find my way back to Maubeuge, and flew off very thankfully, completed my reconnaissance, and landed back at Maubeuge at 5.30." If these proceedings seem strange and amateurish now, it is worth noting that Lieutenant Mapplebeck flew over Brussels itself without recognising it. The result of both reconnaissances was negative: Joubert and Mapplebeck were able to report with assurance on where the Germans were not, but had nothing to say about where they were. However, the R.F.C. was to have plenty of opportunities for improving on this performance, and shortly did so.

Further to the east, around Namur, reconnaissance in another style was being conducted under difficulties. General Sordet's Cavalry Corps, which had entered Belgium on the 6th, had had a trying time since then. Ordered first to link up with the Belgian Army, which became impossible when the latter abruptly retreated to Antwerp on the 18th, it was being used by G.Q.G. as a source of information about the enemy, while General Lanrezac was requesting that it should cover the assembly of his Army. The corps had now been ordered to move to the left flank of the B.E.F. Sordet was a keen officer, who could be depended on to do whatever was possible; the unfortunate fact was that, with the instrument in his hand, not very much was possible at all. The later course of the War made Cavalry unusable, and many sarcastic things have been written about it because of the repeated disasters that occurred when cavalry-minded generals tried to conduct what became essentially siege-warfare in accordance with the requirements of the mounted arm. But August, 1914, had not yet seen that transformation take place; there was still a use for Cavalry, if properly trained and handled. Ironically, it was only the British cavalry, under some of the generals who came in for so much scorn later, that was so trained; the French, despite a gallantry that was even more particularly noticeable in the cavalry than in the rest of their brave Army, were certainly not.

Outward appearances alone were sufficient to convince any informed observer that the French Horse would not be suited to modern war. The troops were excellently mounted, and trained with precision in the traditional cavalry tactics—changing position at a gallop, manœuvring at full speed *en masse*, and above all charging with lance and sabre. But these were Napoleonic methods, survivals of the days of Murat and the pageantry of the Grand Army. The pageantry, indeed, had been retained almost intact. There were regiments of Cuirassiers, big men on powerful horses, who looked almost exactly like the squadrons that had charged at Waterloo. They wore the high, crested helmets, with horse-hair plumes trailing behind, the heavy steel cuirasses, the tall boots of the First Empire. The Dragoons resembled them in all details except that they did not wear the cuirass, and carried lances. The light cavalry were a blaze of colour. The fire-arm of all French cavalry was a wretched little pop-gun that was quite useless on a modern battlefield. The spectacle of a dismounted Cuirassier, trying to use this weapon, was simply ludicrous. Against the German cavalry divisions, recently reorganised to include battalions of Jäger infantry, whose duty was to support the mounted troops with strong fire-power, the French were almost helpless. Whenever they were fortunate enough to come upon the Germans sufficiently quickly to bring them to a mounted action, they did well, and rapidly acquired an ascendancy. It seemed that the knowledge that Infantry were right alongside them did much to reduce the dash of the Kaiser's famous horsemen, who, under his Imperial eye, had been alarming all Europe at their annual manœuvres for some years past. But the German tactics were to draw back upon the Jägers, who, with plentiful machine guns and Horse Artillery, soon brought the French to a standstill. Under these conditions, Sordet could effect little penetration that was worth speaking about, from the point of view of collecting information. And in the attempt to do so, what with the other roles that had been assigned to him, he was rapidly wearing out his Corps. For one final fault of the French cavalry was that it practically never dismounted; saddle sores* and sheer exhaustion had contributed more than casualties in action to reduce the effective strength of Sordet's Corps already by one-sixth.

Even though Sordet and his tired horsemen could provide little of it, information, was, nevertheless, coming into G.Q.G. Some of it was good; some dubious. That from the remoter sources was the best. The Russian Armies had entered Galicia: good. At the Battle of the Jadar, the Serbians had inflicted a sharp reverse on the Austrians invading their country: even better. But the sudden retirement of the Belgians in a direction that took them entirely out of touch with the French, and even with their own fortress of Namur, was alarming. It was the result (though the significance of this was not yet appreciated) of the deployment of von Kluck's Army on the extreme German right. Nearer to hand, General de Langle de Cary, commanding the French 4th Army, reported that large German forces were apparently slipping across his front. He proclaimed that he was ready to attack them while they were still engaged in this flank march westwards. What neither he nor G.Q.G. realised was that these forces, the German Second Army and part of the Third, would soon be replaced opposite de Langle by armies that had not yet been taken into account by the French. This idea, that the extension of the German right wing was being carried out at the expense of their centre, thereby creating a zone of weakness which the French might exploit, was snatched at eagerly by the adherents of Plan XVII. It was to have grave consequences in preventing their eyes from being opened even up to the eleventh hour.

For the time being G.Q.G. was only too glad to accept a favourable interpretation of events on the Allied left, for its real attention was still largely concentrated on the right flank. The advance of the 1st Army in Alsace continued to go forward without difficulty against German forces whose role was deliberately passive. On the 19th the French entered Mulhausen, with loud rejoicings. The 2nd Army in Lorraine, under the crack strategist, General de

* NOTE: Some of the French regiments, it is recorded, smelt dreadful, because of their horses' sore backs.

Castelnau, had been pushing forward for almost a week, and was awaiting the order to begin its final offensive. This was received on the 19th, and great results were anticipated. Nevertheless, Joffre thought it wise on the eve of the offensive, to divert two Army Corps from Castelnau, and send them northwards to take part in the equally stirring events that portended there.

On the German side, the great machine was rolling inexorably forward. The smoothness of its flow across Belgium, the grandiosity of its intentions, its sheer magnitude, can blind us to defects which were as surely at work within it as any on the Allied side. There was, first, a defect of Intelligence. The Germans, engrossed with their own sweeping manœuvres, knew little about their enemies. They had no idea, for example, of the whereabouts of the B.E.F.; they believed that it was only just disembarking, probably at Dunkirk, Calais and Ostend. And secondly, the Chief of Staff, who was, in effect, Commander-in-Chief, was now beginning that series of vacillations and deviations from the Schlieffen Plan which was finally to prove fatal to it. The Sixth and Seventh Armies on the left, both under Crown Prince Rupprecht of Bavaria, were finding their passive role irksome. Prince Rupprecht felt it to be within his powers to inflict a heavy defeat on the French who were advancing towards his prepared positions in Lorraine and Alsace. He asked for permission to counter-attack them, and von Moltke agreed. The results were to prove spectacular in the short run, but ultimately disastrous. The very giving of permission showed that von Moltke's mind was in a state of ominous indecision.

Not so his Imperial master. It was on this day, August 19th, that a famous phrase was coined. From General Headquarters of the German Army at Aix-la-Chapelle, the Kaiser issued to von Kluck the Order which read: "It is my Royal and Imperial Command that you concentrate your energies for the immediate present upon one single purpose, and that is, that you address all your skill and all the valour of my soldiers to exterminate the treacherous English and walk over General French's contemptible* little Army." The B.E.F.

---

* NOTE: "Insignificant" is probably a better rendering of the German; but the "Old Contemptibles" have now secured their place in history. General von Kluck, who appears to have mellowed considerably in later years, subsequently called the B.E.F. "an incomparable army".

was much cheered when it heard of this. The Kaiser might have been cheered, too, had he been able to see the B.E.F. Now coming to the end of its long march to the concentration area, some of the units were looking very strange. About half the men in them had lost, not only their badges, but most of their buttons as well. Pieces of string and tape held the essential parts of their garments together. Many had even parted with their caps, and were wearing horrible civilian substitutes. The word 'souvenir', usually uttered in a high-pitched urchin's bleat, was acquiring a hideous sound.

August 20th was the long-awaited day for the apostles of the French offensive. Believing that the advance in Lorraine and Alsace had now reached the decisive phase, Castelnau, on the 18th, had announced:

> "The enemy is retiring on our front. . . . He must be pursued with the utmost vigour and rapidity.
> "The G.O.C. Second Army relies on the energy of all to achieve this result.
> "He expects corps commanders to instil into their troops the necessary dash, which differs from that required for a methodical advance against prepared positions. . . ."

The fighting on the 19th certainly did not correspond to the conditions suggested in this order. It had none of the character of a 'pursuit'; on the contrary, it was a set battle, in which about half of the French 2nd Army had suffered severe checks, and failed to reach its objectives. The 1st Army had done rather better, though not brilliantly. But the orders still stood, and it was confidently believed that the 20th would see them fulfilled. Castelnau ordered a renewed advance at 5 a.m. against what he believed to be no more than strong rear-guards. To Joffre the situation that morning seemed "in general favourable". At 8.45 he sent a report to the Minister of War. "I felt justified," he says, "in giving it a tone of confidence. But," he wryly adds, "this was going to be the last good news he would get from me for a long time."

During the night of the 19th the German Sixth and Seventh Armies had been assembling for their counter-offensive. Almost immediately after the French left their overnight positions they ran into heavy artillery fire, and then met the German infantry, strongly backed by the inevitable machine guns. The result was a débâcle. It was particularly bad on the front of the 2nd Army which, out of its three active Army Corps, had one well-nigh wrecked, another reduced to an extremely shaky condition, and the third, Foch's XX Corps, intact, but with severe losses. Once again the 1st Army, though also heavily attacked, had not suffered quite so badly; but both Armies, far from pursuing the enemy, were forced to retreat, parts of them in great disorder. By 4 o'clock in the afternoon the news of these defeats, which are known as the Battles of Morhange and Sarrebourg, had reached G.Q.G. All the high hopes of the morning were reduced to dust, but Joffre remained imperturbable. His reaction to the serious news which continued to pour in during the evening was one more of surprise than of alarm. He was aware that something had gone disastrously wrong, but was still far from concluding that the fault might lie with his entire strategy.

He found comfort in the news from his left flank, where the bulk of the 5th Army had reached the line of the Sambre, between Charleroi and Namur. He envisaged the right flank of Lanrezac's Army joining hands with the defenders of this Belgian fortress, which was expected to make an even longer and sterner resistance than Liège. (Joffre was still, incidentally, under the impression that Liège was holding out, although the last fort had surrendered four days earlier.) On Lanrezac's left, Sir John French was able to report that the concentration of the B.E.F. was complete, and that it would be able to advance next day. Much information also came in about German movements in this area, so that, says Joffre, "at the very moment when the Franco-British concentration was being completed, all our previous uncertainty became suddenly dissipated". Unfortunately, uncertainty was only dissipated through yet another exercise in hopeful imagination on the part of G.Q.G.

This was the day on which von Kluck's First Army entered Brussels; their march to the west seemed to indicate that they were in pursuit of the Belgian Army, which had now come to rest in Antwerp. But the report of a British airman of a long column filling the road all the way back into Louvain, coupled with French and Belgian intelligence of more long columns marching westwards in the areas of Wavre and Gembloux, made it clear that the Germans were deploying forces far greater than they would need to dispose of the Belgians. Obviously they were threatening the Allied left wing.

The weight of the threat was still estimated at five or six Army Corps, with three cavalry divisions; in fact, allowing for the detachment from von Bülow's Second Army assigned to the attack on Namur, where the Belgian outposts were in process of being driven in, the Germans were deploying roughly double this strength. But Joffre knew nothing of this, and concluded that: "The movement of the enemy armies with their right wing advanced, would permit us to execute our intended manœuvre, viz., oppose the northern mass with the British and our 5th Army, while with the 3rd and 4th Armies we would attack the German Armies in Luxembourg in a south-north direction, and then, later on, take the northern group of the enemy in flank." His defeat in Lorraine had made him more certain than ever that the German centre must be weak, since both their right and left had now displayed such strength. Accordingly, he ordered the French 3rd and 4th Armies to begin their offensive the next day in the Ardennes sector.

In Lorraine and Alsace the meaning of battle was already known. The scenes of war had already assumed there all the majesty and terror that was shortly to become universal. At Namur, the guns had commenced their thunder. But on the left, where the 5th Army and the British lay, all remained, for a few brief hours longer, quiet. Lieutenant Spears was sitting on one of the hillsides overlooking the Sambre, with a French officer beside him. They were looking out across the great, flat industrial plain to the east of Charleroi. They knew that the enemy were there, but they could see nothing of them. How, they wondered, would the Germans reveal themselves? By what sign?

"The evening was still and wonderfully peaceful. The ominous rumble of guns from the direction of Namur, which had been going on all the afternoon, had ceased. A dog was barking at some sheep. A girl was singing as she walked down the lane behind us. From a little farm away on the right came the voices and laughter of some soldiers cooking their evening meal. Darkness grew in the far distance as the light began to fail.

"Then, without a moment's warning, with a suddenness that made us start and strain our eyes to see what our minds could not realise, we saw the whole horizon burst into flames. To the north, outlined against the sky, countless fires were burning. It was as if hordes of fiends had suddenly been released, and dropping on the distant plain, were burning every town and every village. A chill of horror came over us. War seemed suddenly to have assumed a merciless, ruthless aspect that we had not realised till then."

Sackcloth on the 20th; on the 21st, ashes: on both flanks the French Armies met with serious checks and reverses which belied the high hopes of G.Q.G. On the right, the German pressure against the 1st and 2nd Armies continued; General de Castelnau reported to Joffre: "The situation looks to me very grave, and I feel it my duty to tell you so." He contemplated abandoning Nancy, with its line of fortified heights, and retiring to the Meuse, dividing his Army as he did so. This suggestion, says Joffre, "gave me the greatest concern". He realised what a disastrous moral effect such a retirement would have and urged Castelnau to hang on. Fortunately, as the day wore on, German pressure slackened, and by ten o'clock that night, Joffre's liaison officer with the 2nd Army was able to state that its condition had "materially and morally improved"; Castelnau was still holding on to Nancy; his Army Corps were being reorganised; there was no more talk of retiring behind the Moselle. But there remained the disturbing question, why the 2nd Army had been compelled to retreat so suddenly, under, as Joffre admits, "conditions which almost resembled a rout". It was a question which was on the point of recurring all along the line.

The 3rd and 4th Armies now began their movement into the Ardennes. This hilly, thickly-wooded region, "La Petite Suisse", as it is often called, has always been regarded by the French as one of the major natural obstacles to invasion of their country. It has usually proved a disappointment in this respect; in 1940, for example, the Germans pushed their armour through it with amazing ease. Nevertheless, it is strange and contradictory that G.Q.G. should have considered it a suitable terrain for launching what had now become their main offensive in 1914. The progress of the two Armies through this difficult region was slow and hesitating, although German resistance on the first day was not a serious factor. There was a tendency, from the first, for the French infantry to outpace its artillery and transport. Even on good roads in level country, the

French horse transport of this period was a frightful curse; manned mainly by reservists, it was for ever getting jammed and blocking communications. In the steep, narrow gorges of the Ardennes, its difficulties were multiplied, and with them, those that it caused to the rest of the Armies. However, for the time being, there were no bad reports to G.Q.G. from this area.

To the left, matters were different. The Germans were not risking delays and setbacks at Namur, such as those that they had experienced at Liège. Their attack on the fortress was immediately launched with a fury that daunted the Belgian garrison. A liaison officer from the 5th Army returned to Army Headquarters that night with the impression that the fortress might not even hold out for another day unless heavily reinforced. But General Lanrezac had no intention of diverting any large part of his Army into Namur; not only had he a horror of fortresses in general, but by now those symptoms of despondency which had already been observed in him were becoming acute. It is, of course, not entirely to his discredit, that the nearer he came to the enemy, the more cautious he became. What was disturbing was his silence.

During the afternoon, while Spears was in the 2ème (Intelligence) Bureau of the 5th Army Headquarters at Chimay, General Lanrezac walked in. The Headquarters was lodged in a school building, and in the classroom occupied by the 2ème Bureau a large map hung behind the spot where the master's desk had been. Lanrezac walked up to this map, "unhitched his pince-nez, which were hooked as usual uncomfortably and incongruously behind his ear, where they hung like a pair of cherries, put them on his nose, and began to call out the names of places on the Sambre as he located them with his finger. Then he began to talk in his deep loud voice of what the Germans were doing. He was always interesting when he discoursed like this, for he was a brilliant speaker.

"Presently he went on to talk of the situation of his own Army. We listened intently and respectfully, but he had not been speaking long before my interest changed to amazement and my amazement to incredulity. I could hardly believe my ears as it dawned on me that General Lanrezac was holding forth in eloquent language on the folly of attack."

The gist of Lanrezac's argument was that the 5th Army, now

1 "... *the crowded troopships ... crossed and re-crossed the Channel ...*";
the B.E.F. on its way to France

2 " A khaki-coloured tide flowed out over the docksides . . ."; British troops at Rouen

3 *French*   4 *Wilson*

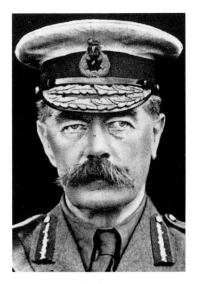

5 *Kitchener*   6 *Smith-Dorrien*

BRITISH COMMANDERS

7 "... the 'kite-held-together-with-string' type ...";
A B.E.2 of No. 2 Squadron, R.F.C.

8 *A German aircraft of 1914*

9 *Joffre*   10 *Lanrezac*

11 *Maunoury*   12 *Franchet d'Esperey*

FRENCH COMMANDERS

13 *"How . . . would the Germans reveal themselves? By what sign?"*

14 *"German . . . patrols were prowling . . ."*

15   *von Kluck*

16   *von Schlieffen*

17   *von Bülow*

18   *von Moltke*

GERMAN COMMANDERS

19 "... as if hordes of fiends ... were burning every town and every village ...";
German troops on the march

lined up along the heights on the south bank of the Sambre, with the steep banks of the Meuse protecting its right flank, would be mad to leave such excellent defensive positions. There was a great deal in what he said. Unfortunately, however, it was wholly at odds with the known intentions of his Commander-in-Chief, whose instructions Lanrezac had now accepted, ostensibly without demur. These instructions had also been accepted by the B.E.F., which was in the very act of conforming to them. Spears, whose duties lay in the co-ordination of the movements of the 5th Army and the B.E.F., became terribly alarmed. "From that moment," he says, "I felt that whatever orders he might receive General Lanrezac would be most unwilling to attack." He went immediately to the Operations Bureau, to ask whether there had been a change of plan; he found that, on the contrary, orders were being drafted to the effect that the 5th Army would "hold itself in readiness to assume the offensive. . . ." But, significantly, the orders continued: "As this offensive is dependent on that of neighbouring armies, the moment when it will take place cannot at the moment be fixed." Joffre had generously agreed that Lanrezac should choose his own moment, since obviously there would be no advantage in committing the 5th Army in isolation. He had not realised that Lanrezac would be disposed to wait for results on other fronts before beginning his own attack. But that was what the word 'dependent' really implied. The disagreeable impression on Spears was so strong that he set out immediately to Le Cateau, to convey his misgivings to French. Unfortunately, he did not meet French himself, or even Murray, but reported to Wilson, who was still on the crest of his optimism.

The information that had been coming into G.H.Q. during the day was not of a kind to warrant optimism. The R.F.C. had observed several German columns, including a large one of all arms at Nivelles, which seemed to be heading straight for the British front. The cavalry had also sighted the enemy, though there had been no engagement, and had collected more news which amply confirmed that of the R.F.C. One such report stated that a German column was moving on Mons from Brussels, and might now be fairly close; this was incorporated in the Intelligence Operation Order of the day. It met with no favour in Wilson's eyes. The Operations Section, over which he presided, even issued a reproof to the Cavalry Division, which read: "The information which you have acquired and conveyed to the Commander-in-Chief appears to be somewhat exaggerated. It is probable that only mounted troops supported by Jägers are in your immediate neighbourhood." Distinctly, this was a case of "whom the Gods wish to destroy. . . ." Henry Wilson did agree with Spears, however, that it would be a good thing for Sir John French and Lanrezac to meet again, so that they might understand each other's minds better.

When Spears returned to 5th Army H.Q., he learned that, so far from beginning its own offensive, the 5th Army had already been heavily attacked. The details were some time in coming in, and it was even longer before they were imparted to G.Q.G. But what had happened was that Lanrezac's III and X Corps, along the Sambre, had been thrown back, and the German Second Army had forced bridgeheads over the river. The excellent defensive positions which Lanrezac had found so alluring earlier in the day had now proved not to be excellent at all. Like any other positions, they needed to be defended resolutely, and this, it soon became clear, had not happened. The troops themselves fought gallantly, but French generalship reached a low ebb on this day. It is worth noting that within a fortnight three out of four divisional commanders, and one of the Corps commanders in these two Army Corps had been replaced. Among them was General Sauret, commander of the III Corps, of whom Joffre recorded that at a critical stage of the battle he was not to be found at all, so that the commander of the Corps artillery had to give orders in his place. Another officer who distinguished himself only in an adverse sense was General Bonnier, commander of the 19th Division in the X Corps, who, according to Lanrezac, was much perturbed when he learned that he had the Prussian Guard in front of him. These Guards certainly fought well; so did some of the French regiments opposed to them. But it would appear that the latter were beaten in their commanders' minds before the fighting began.

The seriousness of the 5th Army's setback was not immediately known; the mood at Army Headquarters was therefore not altogether depressed at the end of the day. Two Corps of the Army, after all, had not been engaged at all. There was still talk of throwing the Germans back into the Sambre next day. But the moral damage, quite apart from the actual losses in battle, inflicted on the III and X

Corps, was to have a lasting effect. This would be felt mainly in the frames of mind of commanders, Lanrezac himself above all. For Joffre, though he did not know it yet, the result of the day's fighting on the 5th Army front was the termination of all his schemes for outflanking the enemy, or breaking through their centre. The one contingency that had never been foreseen was an early retreat by Lanrezac; the latter himself could not known how far-reaching its effects would be. But this day marked the opening of the Battle of Charleroi, itself the first of a series of combats which continued without interruption until mid-September. In that time, the Allied left wing was swept back on a tide of war which flowed down to the Marne, then ebbed again to the Aisne, where the line of battle came to rest in positions which would remain virtually unchanged for the next four years.

All this, however, was hidden in the future. The B.E.F. was marching to Mons with a keenness whetted by the first sight of the enemy, and undimmed by any knowledge of what had befallen its Allies. Henry Wilson wrote, in a letter home: "Today we start our forward march, and the whole line from here to Verdun set out. It is at once a glorious and an awful thought, and by this day week the greatest action that the world has ever heard of will have been fought. I am full of confidence, but nothing is certain in war. . . ."

4

The Eve of Battle

THE B.E.F. was astir very early on the 22nd. The eyes and finger-tips of the Army were General Allenby's Cavalry Division, stretched in a wide arc well ahead of the main infantry bodies. "C" Squadron of the 4th Dragoon Guards, under Major Bridges, had spent the night in a wood beside the main road that leads from Mons to Brussels through Soignies. Bridges was hoping to be able to ambush some of the enemy's advance-guard, in order to identify German formations in front of the B.E.F. Daylight, however, brought no sign of the enemy, so he decided to push on with his squadron and look for them. He did not have far to go. Very soon the Germans came into view—four cavalrymen riding down the road, very suspicious and wary. Something alarmed them, and they turned back. Lieutenant Hornby pleaded with Bridges to be allowed to chase them, and Bridges let him go, with two troops of the squadron, following on himself with the remainder at a trot.

"The Uhlans,* a squadron, took to their heels and the chase went merrily down the hard high road, fortunately a very wide one for about a mile and a half. We caught them up in the village of Soignies where there was a regular mêlée. The Uhlans were hampered by their long lances and a good many threw them away. Several were killed, Hornby for one running his man through.

"The skirmish was over by the time I arrived and the Uhlans,

---

* Actually the 4th Cuirassiers of the 9th Cavalry Division. All German cavalry carried lances in 1914, and were therefore liable to be lumped together as Uhlans, even by those who should have known better. Uhlans were Lancers proper, and were distinguished by the famous square-topped helmet, very similar to the full-dress headgear of Lancers in the British Army. The German Dragoons and Cuirassiers wore the *pickelhaube*, with spikes of varying ornateness.

joined by two troops of Hussars which had arrived by a by-road, were again in flight pursued by the relentless Hornby. But soon, on mounting a hill, the chase was brought to an end by sharp rifle-fire from a battalion of cyclists in position on the crest."

Bridges immediately dismounted his squadron, and the Germans had their first taste of what the British cavalry could do on foot, which was as unpalatable to them as its behaviour when mounted. They were quite happy to let the 4th Dragoon Guards go away un-molested when orders came for them, a little later, to withdraw and move, with the rest of the Cavalry Division, to the left flank of the Army. This brief action was significant, not only because it was the first encounter between British troops and the Germans in the First World War, but because it instantly answered a question that had been present, if unspoken, in many minds. "We did not quite know what would happen," says Bridges, "when we got up against the German cavalry of which there were great masses all trained to shock action. But Hornby had solved the problem for us, and when Uhlan prisoners, captured Prussian horses and a stack of lances in a buggy were brought in by the Squadron Sergeant-major past the whole Cavalry Division, there was no further doubt and "C" Squadron was greeted with a well-deserved cheer on its return." Lieutenant Hornby received the D.S.O. for his part in the affair. Later in the day other regiments performed equally satisfactory exploits. Two squadrons of the Scots Greys succeeded in persuading the enemy that they were a whole brigade, mainly through the accuracy of their dismounted rifle-fire. A troop of the 16th Lancers had the satis-faction of riding down a party of Jägers. It was a good day for the British cavalry. They carried the Lee-Enfield infantry rifle, and showed that they could use it without losing a particle of their dash in the saddle.

Besides effectively screening the movements of the B.E.F. from the enemy's view, the cavalry were able to supply G.H.Q. with a considerable amount of useful information—useful, that is, if it had been heeded. But Intelligence from British sources was still under a handicap. Before his squadron withdrew, Bridges had come to the conclusion that strong enemy forces were coming down from the north against the front of the B.E.F., and reported accordingly. Other cavalry patrols confirmed this impression, but their views made little impact on G.H.Q. "I have sometimes wondered," remarks Bridges, with understandable sourness, "why (French) should not have believed and acted upon the information obtained by his cavalry." But it was not only the cavalry that had this curious psychological obstacle to contend with. The Royal Flying Corps was very active. It flew off twelve reconnaissances from Maubeuge, all of which helped to reveal the enemy's movements and the presence of large masses of his troops in front of the British. The most important of these reconnaissances observed a long German column, estimated at an Army Corps,* marching along the road from Brussels to Ninove, that is, almost due west, and then, at Ninove, turning down towards Grammont, south-westwards, a well-defined wheel which would bring them *outside* the British left flank. The importance of this report was immediately recognised at R.F.C. Headquarters, and Brigadier-General Sir David Henderson, commanding the R.F.C., took it personally to G.H.Q. Nevertheless, what finally influenced French's mind was not this volume of conclusive information from his own sources but that which came in to him later from the French.

On their side, the only good news of the day was from the front where there was no news—or very little. German activity against the 1st and 2nd Armies was on a reduced scale; further small withdrawals were made by both Armies, but there was no crisis. In the Ardennes it was a different story. There the 3rd and 4th Armies experienced in their turn precisely similar misfortunes to those which had befallen the French in Alsace and Lorraine two days previously. Both Armies had run into stiff German resistance and counterattacks which had not merely checked their own offensive but in places thrown them back. The terrible realisation began to dawn that the whole French military machine was being found inadequate to the stresses of modern war. Its training, its equipment, its very clothing, all were wrong. The French infantry of those days were still dressed in the red *képis*, the long dark-blue *capotes* (greatcoats), and the red trousers of the Second Empire. They did not look markedly different from the men who had stormed Sebastopol in 1855. They marched under a heavy load of personal equipment which towered up on their shoulders, so that on the march they always seemed to be leaning forward, bowed by fatigue. Their

* Note: The II Corps, of the First Army.

marching powers were, in truth, remarkable. Straggling along in loose formation, all over the roads, all out of step, they were a startling sight to English observers; but they usually "got there", all the same. Mainly recruited from workers on the soil, this French infantry, as well as displaying great physical stamina, revealed a stoicism, a capacity for endurance in defeat that astonished its own leaders; indeed, it took them some time to bring themselves to believe in it.

It was a tragedy that these excellent qualities should have been dissipated as they were in the early battles of 1914. The doctrine of the headlong offensive had much to answer for; at the tactical level it had come to be interpreted as an injunction to all troops to hurl themselves at the enemy on sight, without waiting for support or the co-ordination of all arms on the battlefield, which is the very essence of generalship. "The sense of the tragic futility of it will never quite fade," says Spears, who was with them, "from the minds of those who saw these brave men, dashing across the open to the sound of drums and bugles, clad in the old red caps and trousers which a parsimonious democracy dictated they should wear, although they turned each man into a target. The gallant officers who led them were entirely ignorant of the stopping power of modern firearms, and many of them thought it chic to die in white gloves." The casualties were terrible. It is known that in August alone the French lost some ten per cent of their officer corps, and their total casualty figure for the month was over 200,000. The only relieving feature of these disastrous encounters was the evident quality of the French Field Artillery, the famous '75s, whenever it was handled properly. These admirable quick-firers, of which the French had large numbers, quickly dominated their German counterparts, and struck fear into the German infantry. On the other hand, the German mobile Heavy Artillery, especially their 5.9 howitzers, produced effects that the French could not equal. And in the close country of the Ardennes, even the '75s were at a disadvantage. In some of the Army Corps of the 3rd and 4th Armies there were routs among the shattered infantry as alarming as those which had already occurred at Morhange and Saarebourg.

It was soon clear that there would be no help from the quarter of the 3rd and 4th Armies for General Lanrezac, himself in difficulties on the Sambre. The fortress of Namur was still holding out, though its prospects were bleak indeed, with the German siege-train of 42-cm. howitzers now in action. Attempted counter-attacks by the French III and X Corps, designed to regain the ground lost on the previous day, not merely failed but resulted in further retreats. Some of the units fell into great confusion. An air of gloom descended on the Army Headquarters. Reports from the front were sparse, and slow to arrive. All the difficulties of communication between the firing line and the command posts in the rear, which were to cause such havoc throughout the war, were now being experienced for the first time. The strain of waiting, while the sound of the guns drew steadily nearer, told heavily on General Lanrezac and his Staff, at their Advanced Headquarters at Mettet. It was not relieved by incidents such as the following*:

"Several of the Staff were standing in the street, when a motor-car drove up coming from the north. It proceeded slowly round the Place towards the church steps on which General Lanrezac was standing. In it reclined a badly wounded man, with a face the colour of ashes. On seeing General Lanrezac he made a sign, and the car stopped. Many officers recognised General Boé, commanding the 20th Division belonging to the X Corps. The wounded man made another sign. His hand lifted as if to salute, but dropped and hung over the door. General Lanrezac did not move. He turned to Hély d'Oissel, who was standing by him, and said, 'You go and talk to him.' The Chief of Staff stepped quickly forward, almost ran to the car, and clasped Boé's hand. He did not speak. Boé was silent for a moment, looking towards Lanrezac. Then he whispered, 'Tell him. . . .' he gasped, then, speaking louder as he realised Hély d'Oissel could hardly hear him, he repeated, 'Tell the general we held on as long as we could.' His head fell back, his eyes were very sad. Hély d'Oissel grasped his hand again and said nothing. Still General Lanrezac had not moved. The car grated into gear, and drove slowly on."

The realisation that matters were so serious at the front that a divisional commander had been severely wounded by rifle-fire did not cheer the spectators of this incident.

* Spear, *Liaison.*

General Lanrezac sustained his gloomy vigil at Mettet, some distance ahead of his actual Army Headquarters at Chimay. In one respect this displacement was most unfortunate, for during the morning Sir John French, having set his own Army in motion, decided to visit Lanrezac again to discover how events were progressing on his right. Quite by accident, in the course of one of his frequent journeys along the line, Spears encountered French's motor-car. The C.-in-C. signalled him to stop, and, under the eyes of some suspicious French infantry who were halted along the road, the British Staff Officers entered a cottage, half estaminet, to confer. Just as they had spread out their maps on one of the tables, and Spears was about to recount to Sir John what he knew of the 5th Army's position, the lady of the house, who had gazed at their entry open-mouthed, resumed washing up her dishes in a tub, making such a frightful clatter that no one could hear himself speak. This was dealt with, not without difficulty, and Spears was able to repeat to French what he had already told Wilson—that Lanrezac was in neither the mood nor the position to undertake the offensive on which British plans were based. He added a further warning that the B.E.F. might shortly be facing a grave threat to its left flank, basing himself on the information which had been received by the 2ème Bureau of 5th Army. French appeared to be impressed. Spears may have done some good in preparing his mind for the news that reached him later in the day; for the time being, however, French made no change in his dispositions, nor in the orders to his Army.

The end of the meeting left Spears with a sense of personal failure. He was extremely eager for French and Lanrezac to meet again, and here was French, on his way to such a meeting. But when he learned that Lanrezac was at Mettet, he decided that it was too far away for him to go. Spears pleaded with him to continue, and meet the commander of the 5th Army, but French was adamant. "Perhaps I was not emphatic enough," says Spears. "I was only a subaltern, and much intimidated at having to deal with such important people. The glamour of the great still dazzled me, and I failed to gain my point." It was a serious misfortune, though Spears cannot be blamed for it. It is not really the function of a junior liaison officer to tell a Commander-in-Chief how he should act. The fault lay in the disastrous first meeting between French and Lanrezac. French was already taking the initiative in seeking another meeting; but the desire for it was probably not strong enough to support the extra trouble involved by Lanrezac's removal to Mettet, in view of the high probability that the meeting itself would be disagreeable, and might contain further insulting behaviour. At any rate, French returned immediately to Le Cateau, pondering, no doubt, on the information that Spears had given him.

The news of the setbacks sustained all along the left of his line did not reach Joffre until the end of the day. He only received the details of what happened in the Ardennes, at what were later called the Battles of Virton and the Semoy, the following morning. Lanrezac's report was telephoned to G.Q.G. at 8.30 p.m. Other worries, however, were beginning to afflict the French Commander-in-Chief. The Government was becoming alarmed at the increasing reports of German cavalry advancing well to the west, threatening Lille and Roubaix. In this area, covering the whole distance from the left wing of the B.E.F. to the English Channel, there were only three Territorial divisions and the garrison of Lille. Joffre ordered up another Territorial division to stiffen this thin and fragile screen. Meanwhile, General Sordet's Cavalry Corps was in the process of passing, via the rear of the B.E.F., to the left flank. Its movements were slow and impeded. Somewhat unjustly, Joffre began to wonder whether Sordet was up to his task. It would be a long time before G.Q.G. properly appreciated the conditions under which some of its subordinate formations were operating, and the difficulties which beset them. At G.Q.G., although a great deal of their fatuous optimism had now evaporated, enough remained to produce much impatience with struggling officers like Sordet. Still snatching at encouragement, wherever it was offered, Joffre was delighted to learn that the Russians had now entered East Prussia, and that twenty-eight of their Army Corps were in contact with the enemy. Understandably, he supposed that this advance might soon produce a useful reaction on his own front. In due course it did, but there was much to be suffered in the interval.

German Supreme Headquarters, for their part, were still operating largely in the dark. Encounters with the British cavalry, and the shooting down of a British aeroplane, revealed that the B.E.F. was present, but the complete failure of the German cavalry to penetrate the screen of Allenby's division left unanswered the questions: in what strength the B.E.F. had arrived, and from what bases it was operating. Such was the German ignorance in these matters that their First Army, now in the full process of its great turning movement on the right, halted for two hours during the morning, and prepared to face westward, under the impression that the B.E.F. was detraining at Tournai. Only when von Kluck realised that it was a French Territorial division that had been seen there did the advance of the First Army continue. These two wasted hours were to have a serious effect on his battle with the British next day. Meanwhile, on his left, von Bülow was pressing the French hard, and, to the left of him again, von Hausen's Saxon Third Army was making its presence felt. The approach of this Army, entirely unsuspected by the French, had a profound effect on the results of the day.

Severely pressed by the German Second Army's frontal attacks on the Sambre, and with many units now in a disorganised condition, the 5th Army had yielded more ground all along its line. Both its flanking corps, the I Corps on the right, and the XVIII Corps on the left, were, however, still intact, and there seemed a reasonable prospect of at least bringing the Germans to a standstill. This hope became very much fainter during the afternoon, when the presence of the German XII Saxon Corps was reported on the Meuse, near Dinant, threatening the right flank of the 5th Army. The Saxons began immediately to push bridgeheads over the river; but their operations on this and the following days were characterised by a certain lack of vigour, in marked contrast to those of the First and Second Armies. The French had little difficulty in holding them on the 22nd. Nevertheless, the threat itself was decisive. General Lanrezac concluded that he must continue his retreat, and reported accordingly to Joffre.

Spears saw at once that this decision opened up fearful prospects for the B.E.F. Already he was acutely conscious of the threat to its left flank; the day's movements would bring the B.E.F. some 9 miles forward of the 5th Army, with a wide gap between them; further retirement by the French would expose the B.E.F. to an attack on the right flank too, with every likelihood of envelopment and destruction.

Once again, he set off post-haste to Le Cateau with a dire warning. It had been a gruelling day, and the drive was a distressing one, through the encumbered back areas of the 5th Army, along roads which, besides the military transport, were now filling with pitiful throngs of refugees, Belgian and French, fleeing before the brutalities of the German advance. These wretched people were to prove a serious menace both to the mobility and to the safety of the Armies; but at this stage there was nothing to be done about them. They presented a problem that was quite new, another indication of the special quality of horror that the War was assuming. Shocked and distraught, heavily-laden, pushing and pulling pathetic carts and perambulators stacked with their household goods, dressed in their best clothes, dragging their children with them, the only misery they lacked was that of being machine-gunned and dive-bombed from the air, as their descendants were in 1940. Spears arrived at Le Cateau exhausted, and was more than grateful to meet Colonel Macdonogh, Head of British Intelligence, who led him away immediately in the direction of a half-bottle of champagne which he had set by.

Macdonogh and Spears then went to find French, who was at dinner; but he did not keep them waiting long. The Commander-in-Chief and General Murray listened grimly to what Spears had to tell them. Then he and Macdonogh were told to wait in an ante-room while the generals reflected. The scene in that room fixed itself in his mind: "Round the table, the empty coffee cups pushed out of the way to make room for maps, the Chiefs of Staff of the two Corps and of the cavalry, with one or two officers of the Commander-in-Chief's personal staff, were in animated conversation. A sickly feeling came over me as I realised that they were discussing a plan, evidently already decided upon, for a general advance upon the following day. Representatives of neighbouring units were perfecting details, arranging communications, fixing time-tables, making notes in field service books. They paid no attention to the two individuals sitting on the sofa, whose mood was so strikingly different from theirs. Round the table keenness, suppressed excitement, joy and confidence, sparkled through the ordinary technical conversation of these men who already saw themselves marching to victory on the morrow, whilst we in our corner knew that their hopes must be dashed, that the advance we had all dreamed of would not take place, that, perhaps before it could even strike a blow at the enemy, the Army, *our* Army, might be forced to retire." Once again a hideous sense of personal responsibility came over Spears; he found himself thinking of Captain Nolan at Balaklava, whose misconceived interpretation of a general's intentions had caused the disaster to the Light Brigade. It was a nasty position for a subaltern.

Sir John French did not take long to make up his mind. General Murray returned to the room, and said to the officers round the table: "You are to come in now and see the Chief. He is going to tell you that there will be no advance. But remember there are to be no questions. Don't ask why. There is no time and it would be useless. You are to take your orders, that's all. Come on in now." They followed Murray in; Spears had completed his day's work.

The story was not quite ended, however. Later that night an officer appeared from General Lanrezac, bringing the request that the B.E.F. should, on the next day, attack in flank the Germans who were pressing the 5th Army. This was an extraordinary demand, made no more intelligible by Lanrezac's simultaneous report to Joffre that the B.E.F. was, at this time, "Still in echelon to the rear of the 5th Army"—a position which, if true, would have made it quite impossible for the British to do as he asked them. "In view of the most probable situation of the German Army, as it was known to both of us," remarked French, "and the palpable intention of its commander to effect a great turning movement round my left flank . . . it is very difficult to realise what was in Lanrezac's mind when he made such a request to me. . . ." However, with a loyalty that did him credit, even if we may now suspect that it was largely attributable to the remains of his first optimism, and a lingering unwillingness to believe in the full extent of the danger that threatened him, French agreed to remain in his present position for twenty-four hours.

That position, which some units of the Cavalry Division and the I Corps only reached at 3 a.m. the following morning, after long and trying marches under a blazing sun, was the battlefield of Mons. It was anything but an ideal ground for fighting a defensive battle; it had not, of course, been chosen for such a purpose—it just happened to be the point at which the Army halted in the advance that never came off.

5

Mons

THE REGION which contains the battlefield of Mons is one of the dreariest in Western Europe. Mons itself, the capital of Hainault, with a population of some 28,000 in 1914, is a reasonably compact and not entirely unattractive town, as industrial centres go. But beside it sprawl the drab mining villages of the coal belt of which it is the centre; an almost continuous built-up area stretches some 16 miles to the west, bisected by the Mons–Condé Canal. This Canal, running perfectly straight on a directly east–west line, marked the front along which the B.E.F. was mainly engaged on August 23rd. It was an unsatisfactory position in every way. The approaches to it from the north were masked by the cluster of hamlets, the rows of houses and factories and the slag-heaps which filled the valley. A complex drainage system, with a labyrinth of artificial water-courses and osier-beds, varied on the higher ground by woods and spinneys, fringed the Canal, making both movement and vision extremely difficult for the troops stationed along it. Never more than 7 feet deep, with an average width of 64 feet, crossed by eighteen bridges in the course of its 16 miles length, the Canal itself presented no obstacle worth speaking of to troops wishing to cross it, but every impediment to those who would seek to defend it. Indeed, without any such intention, they would be writing a new chapter in the history of war, for this was the first time that great armies had come into conflict in a highly developed European industrial area. For the unfortunate and unprepared inhabitants of this swarming district— numbers of them, including many children, were caught on their way to early Mass, when the battle opened, and holiday trains were still running—the day was a nightmare of noise and destruction.

It was General Smith-Dorrien's II Army Corps which lined the

Canal, facing north, from the bridge at Le Petit Crepin to the west, to the bridge at Obourg, some 3 miles east of Mons. The bridges, of course, shaped the day's fighting, and determined its rigid, repetitive quality. Smith-Dorrien's left flank was guarded by the newly formed independent 19th Infantry Brigade, which linked up in turn with the French 84th Territorial Division. The 5th Division, under Major-General Sir Charles Fergusson, held the main Canal line; the 3rd Division, under Major-General Hubert Hamilton, held the right of the front, including the town of Mons and the awkward salient to the north-east of it, where the Canal runs round Mons into the River Sambre. From the first it was realised that this salient, which included the town bridges, the railways bridges to the north of them, and two more important bridges at Nimy and Obourg, would be the danger-point for the British defence. Almost at right angles to the front of the II Corps, linking with it just south-east of Mons, and running across to the left flank of the French Fifth Army, with which it was

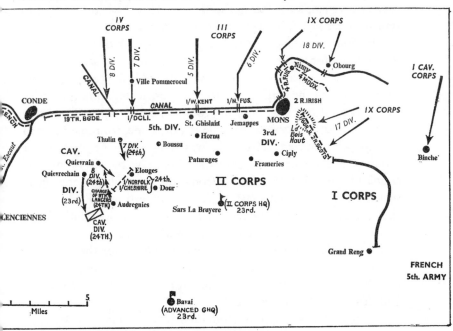

The Battle of Mons, August 23rd, and rearguard actions on August 24th
(Dots beside place-names are only tokens and do not indicate size. A continuous built-up area stretched from Mons to Condé)

in only tenuous contact, came Haig's I Corps, facing almost due east. The 5th Cavalry Brigade was also on this flank; the remaining four cavalry brigades, under Allenby, were behind the 5th Division, on the left of the Army.

To Smith-Dorrien's Headquarters, in the Château of Sars la Bruyère, came a stream of early visitors. Sir John French had selected this place to meet the two Corps commanders and General Allenby to confer about the day's operations. French's outlook had apparently undergone one of those bewildering spontaneous readjustments which were to cause such perplexity to all those who had dealings with him in the days to come. According to Smith-Dorrien, he was "in excellent form, and told us to be prepared to move forward, or to fight where we were, but to get ready for the latter by strengthening our outposts and preparing the bridges over the Canal for demolition". French informed his subordinate commanders that "little more than one, or at most two, enemy Corps, with perhaps a cavalry division, were facing the B.E.F." How he had managed to return to this belief, in view of the information that he had received the previous day, is a mystery. The plausible speech of Henry Wilson may account for it, for Wilson was still clinging to the same idea that afternoon, when two German Corps were already fully engaged, with a third entering the battle and a fourth approaching. Smith-Dorrien was somewhat less sanguine, and took the opportunity of pointing out the unsatisfactory nature of the II Corps line, from the point of view of a protracted defence. It was not only the nature of the ground, but the extent of it that worried him: his two divisions were stretched out along 21 miles of front—an impossible alignment in which to resist a serious attack. Already he had examined a much shorter, and somewhat better position some 2 miles south of the Canal, which would exclude the town of Mons and the salient beside it. He told French that he was preparing orders for the advanced troops to retire to this line "as soon as things got so hot as to risk their being cut off". It seemed to Smith-Dorrien that French agreed with his views, "and approved my action".

No such agreement appears from French's subsequent recollections of the day. On the contrary, their tone is distinctly critical of Smith-Dorrien. French himself issued no written orders between 11.55 p.m. on August 21st and 8.25 p.m. on August 24th, so there is nothing official with which to confirm or deny either view. But it is an inescapable conclusion that, from the moment this conference ended, French's contact with, and control over the actual day-to-day fighting of his Army became more and more shadowy. G.H.Q. acquires an air of functioning on another plane than that of the commanders and soldiers facing the enemy. In any case, after the conference French left immediately for Valenciennes, where he inspected the 19th Infantry Brigade, and talked to the French commander there. He did not return to his own headquarters until the afternoon, by which time his Army had been engaged in its first battle of the Great War for over six hours. It seems an odd performance. One would have expected the swelling roar of gunfire to have brought the Commander-in-Chief back to the centre of things as rapidly as possible; indeed, the bombardment was already lively before he left, which makes his departure seem even more curious.

While the generals were still in conference, the first skirmishes of the day had begun. It was a misty dawn, with a drizzle of rain, but by 10 o'clock the sun was out again. The divisional cavalry of the I Corps, reconnoitring east of Mons, were soon driven in, and by 6 a.m. German cavalry had reached the salient, and were exchanging shots with the 4th Middlesex Regiment, covering the bridge at Obourg. More German horsemen quickly appeared all along the line from Obourg in the east to the bridge facing Ville Pommeroeul in the west, the extreme left flank of the II Corps. Very shortly, from prisoners and the uniforms of the enemy dead, the presence of two German Army Corps, the III and the IX, had been established, together with the 9th Cavalry Division, belonging to their II Cavalry Corps—and all these formations bearing directly on the front of the two divisions of Smith-Dorrien's Corps. On Haig's front all was quiet.

It was a curious battle that was now about to flare into action. The British Commander-in-Chief had absented himself from it at an early stage, and played no perceptible part in it when he returned. The German Commander, Generaloberst von Kluck, seems to have exercised just as little control. He knew next to nothing about the dispositions of the British Army, and his own Army Corps were permitted to stumble into it one by one as they arrived, with no co-ordination of their activities at all. The first to come up was the IX Corps, on the German left, striking into the northern and eastern faces of the salient. Before 9 a.m. the guns of this Corps were in position on the high ground north of the Canal and had began to pour a concentrated fire into the salient, over which they had complete observation. Brigadier-General Doran's 8th Infantry Brigade had been ordered to make a "stubborn resistance", and well they did so. Half the brigade, the 1st Gordon Highlanders and the 2nd Royal Scots, were drawn up on the high ground behind Mons, facing eastwards. The 4th Middlesex held the salient itself, with the 2nd Royal Irish Regiment in close support. The 4th Royal Fusiliers of the 9th Brigade prolonged the line, round the west face of the salient and through the town. By 9 a.m. the infantry of the German 18th Division (IX Corps) were pressing forward against the whole curve between Obourg and Nimy.

Immediately, the fighting assumed the character that it was to retain all through the day. The British troops had been on their position since the evening of the 22nd, and had automatically set about digging themselves in among the houses and the slag-heaps. It was no easy matter to construct trenches, or to lay them out to give a reasonable field of fire on this close terrain; the slag-heaps seemed to offer good observation points, but usually it turned out that these were commanded from other, higher heaps, or they were too hot to stand on. The artillery found conditions especially trying, and many batteries were held in the rear, while those that did go forward had, in some cases, to split up into sections, or even operate single guns. But what could be done, the infantry did; the 1st Royal West Kents at St. Ghislain, for example, were able to construct excellent trenches giving a good field of fire over the water-courses fringing the Canal. Elsewhere it was more difficult, but along its entire length the thin British outpost line was well-concealed. Troops under fire feel naked, and under the deluge of shells that fell upon them, with German aircraft overhead spotting for their artillery (a practice not yet adopted in the British Army), most of the soldiers felt anything but concealed as the day wore on. But the dominating German impression was the uncanny one of facing an invisible enemy, who might be anywhere, and who might equally vanish as soon as one spotted him, to turn up again in another unexpected place shortly afterwards. As late as noon, one regiment of the German III Corps arrived at Baudour, 2 miles north of the Canal, and was told that there was no enemy within 50 miles—(in which case, they might have asked themselves, what on earth was all the shooting about?)—and then, almost immediately afterwards, two Hussars galloped past them, covered in blood, shouting that the enemy were just in front. British tactics, schooled by Boer marksmanship, proved distinctly superior to those of the Continental Armies.

It was infantry shooting that dominated the day. The Germans, as they reached the British positions, pushed home their attacks in a fashion that astounded the regimental officers and soldiers facing them. Their uniforms were not as conspicuous as those of the French; there was less of flying colours, blowing bugles and beating drums; but the target they presented was just as obvious. "They were in solid square blocks, standing out sharply against the skyline," said one British sergeant, "and you couldn't help hitting them. . . . We lay in our trenches with not a sound or sign to tell them of what was before them. They crept nearer and nearer, and then our officers gave the word. . . . They seemed to stagger like a drunk man hit suddenly between the eyes, after which they made a run for us, shouting some outlandish cry that we couldn't make out. . . ." "Poor devils of infantry!" said a Gordon Highlander. "They advanced in companies of quite 150 men in files five deep, and our rifle has a flat trajectory up to 600 yards. Guess the result. We could steady our rifles on the trench and take deliberate aim. The first company were simply blasted away to Heaven by a volley at 700 yards, and in their insane formation every bullet was almost sure to find two billets. The other companies kept advancing very slowly, using their dead comrades as cover, but they had absolutely no chance. . . ." When the Germans tried to form a firing line close to the British positions, says the sergeant, "a few of the crack shots were told off to indulge in independent firing. . . . That is another trick taught us by Brother Boer, and our Germans did not like it at all."

The British, for their part, did not greatly care for the attentions of the German artillery. The First World War was very soon to become mainly an artillery war, with the infantry of both sides in the dismal role of cannon-fodder. There was nothing in this gun-fire at Mons to equal the great barrages of later years. But the impression, on troops who had never experienced anything like it, of this first encounter with German massed batteries, was a vivid and unforgettable one. "God! How their artillery do fire!" said the Gordon Highlander. "We were in the trenches waiting for them," an anonymous wounded soldier told *The Times*, "but we didn't expect anything like the smashing blow that struck us. All at once, so it seemed, the sky began to rain down bullets and shells. At first the shells went very wide, for their fire was bad, but after a time—I think it was a long time—they got our range and then they fairly mopped us up. I saw shells bursting to right and left of me and I saw many a good comrade go out." A Royal Field Artillery officer noted in his diary: "W. Kents, Middlesex and Northumberlands decimated by shell-fire." The word 'decimated' came to have a more literal meaning later; only one of the three battalions that he mentioned had casualties that would be considered severe in November, at Ypres, or even three days later, at Le Cateau. But on this broken ground, where it was difficult enough to see anything at the best of times, when the German shells thundered down and threw up clouds of smoke in every direction, it was impossible to know what was happening elsewhere along the line, and too easy to suppose the worst. The conviction grew that the enemy's artillery was doing terrible damage. And out of this conviction, superstition was quickly born. It seemed to this Royal Artillery officer that the German guns were finding their targets surprisingly quickly. "There is no doubt," he wrote, "that it was mainly due to the amazingly efficient secret service of the enemy." No doubt the Germans, as the British 18-pounders showered them with devastating shrapnel, or the heavies searched their back areas with 60-lb. high-explosive shells, were saying the same thing. But from this moment onwards the B.E.F. would waste an extraordinary amount of time and energy, looking for non-existent spies, and numbers of innocent people would be shot before a proper scepticism set in.

The German 18th Division pressed home its attacks against the salient with great courage. The Middlesex Regiment and the Royal Fusiliers pumped their bullets into the enemy masses ceaselessly; the machine-gun section of the Royal Irish came up to help them, and after a time the Germans appeared to realise the futility of their tactics. Breaking up into small parties, they worked their way over the Canal, and began to infiltrate round the flanks of the Middlesex. The fighting at this stage became very confused in the salient; casualties were increasing in the British battalions; communication began to be a problem, under the rain of shells; but there was no sign that the "stubborn resistance" of the 8th Brigade and the Fusiliers had been at all seriously impaired.

Further to the left, as the morning wore on, the main body of the German III Corps came into action against the remainder of the 9th Brigade and the 5th Division. These units, drawn up along the straight line of the Canal, had only the difficulties of observation to contend with; they were not subjected to an enveloping fire from three sides like their comrades on the right. The 1st Royal Scots Fusiliers and the 1st Northumberland Fusiliers were the first to meet the new attack, by the German 6th Division, just west of Mons. At Mariette, $3\frac{1}{2}$ miles along the Canal, the Northumberlands were amazed to see a German column swinging down towards the bridge in fours. They soon put a stop to this, and then, when the Germans deployed and came on again, ambushed them neatly against a barricade and a wire entanglement. Falling back with heavy casualties, the German infantry now paused while two guns were brought up to demolish the Fusiliers' defences. No sooner was this done than the Northumberlands had another shock: instead of German infantry advancing against them, they saw a crowd of little Belgian schoolgirls coming down the road. Naturally they held their fire, and the enemy, taking advantage of this, rushed forward to out-flank the British outposts, which then had to be withdrawn across the Canal. There is no knowing how this incident arose. It may have been a deliberate act on the part of the Germans—their general behaviour in Belgium was bad enough to make anything possible. On the other hand, the sudden opening of the battle and the total unpreparedness of the civil population make it equally possible that these children were simply, like many other unfortunate people, caught between the lines, and trying a dash for it. After forty years, it should be possible to give the Germans the benefit of the doubt; their performance in the interval, however, makes it difficult to do so.

Once across the Canal, the Northumberlands had little difficulty in bringing the German attack to a standstill again. To their left, at St. Ghislain, the 1st Royal West Kents, in their well-prepared trenches, scored a considerable success against the Brandenburg Grenadiers of the German 5th Division. The enemy attacked first with the Fusilier battalion of the regiment, which was met by a shattering fire. The remaining two battalions then deployed, and slowly drove in the outpost line of the West Kents. One platoon fought its way out of encirclement, with the enemy only 100 yards away. Four guns of the 120th Battery, Royal Field Artillery, which had been sited on the towpath of the Canal itself, after doing much execution, were compelled to withdraw as the German infantry came closer; but the attack finally came to a halt 300 yards from the Canal. The Germans were convinced that the British had brought into action great numbers of machine guns; they had never dreamt of anything like the "mad minute" of concentrated rifle-fire which the British infantry had perfected—sixteen aimed rounds in a minute was quite usual, and some prodigious experts could work up to thirty. The novelist Walter Bloem commanded a company in the Brandenburg regiment. That evening his battalion commander said to him: "You are my sole and only support . . . you are the only company commander left in the battalion . . . the battalion is a mere wreck, my proud, beautiful battalion!" Bloem commented: "Our first battle is a heavy, an unheard-of heavy, defeat, and against the English, the English we laughed at."

It was the same story everywhere. To the left of the West Kents, at Les Herbières, the German 52nd Infantry Regiment began well by dribbling men in small parties up to the Canal bank to drive in the 2nd King's Own Scottish Borderers. Then, after a short bombardment, the same regiment attacked the railway bridge, held by the 1st East Surrey Regiment, with two battalions in mass. The fate of these two battalions was the same as that of every German massed attack; they were shot to pieces, and decisively repulsed, with small casualties to the East Surreys. All in all, it had been a good morning's work. Smith-Dorrien's two divisions had more than held their own against the four German divisions that had so far been brought against them. Indeed, not more than seven or eight British battalions out of the twenty-four in II Corps had been seriously engaged, while the I Corps had been left entirely untroubled. However, it was more clear than ever that the crux of this battle lay, for the II Corps, in the salient, where conditions promised soon to become very difficult. For the B.E.F. as a whole, the crux lay further to the east, where General Lanrezac's 5th Army was finding the third day of the Battle of Charleroi as disagreeable as its beginning.

The centre of the 5th Army, much shaken and disorganised by the fighting of the last two days, spent the morning of the 23rd in that well-known exercise which is so often mentioned to explain a retreat, 're-grouping'. It was fortunate that General Lanrezac's opponent, sixty-eight-year-old Generaloberst von Bülow, was a cautious commander, famous in pre-war manœuvres for his careful 'shoulder-to-shoulder' tactics, which laid great stress on the dangers of units moving without elaborate mutual support. A bolder man might have broken Lanrezac's centre on this day; instead, through extreme deliberation and faulty information, von Bülow exposed himself to what could have been a very disruptive local counter-attack.

While the French III and X Corps were trying to re-organise, their I Corps, on the right, and lying well forward of its neighbours, found itself presented with a unique opportunity. This Army Corps was unquestionably the best in Lanrezac's command. Its general, Franchet d'Esperey, proved to be one of the outstanding French leaders of the war. Short, square, dynamic and resolute, d'Esperey brought to the execution of the French offensive doctrine not only the aggressive spirit without which it became merely a mockery but a clear-headed professional capacity for planning and carrying out attacks. These were rare qualities at his level of command in the French Army at this period. By 10 a.m. on August 23rd a situation had developed which promised the fullest scope for his talents. Suddenly it was realised that the German Guard Corps, on the left of von Bülow's line, was advancing straight across the front of d'Esperey's Corps, presenting its flank 'wide open' to a destructive blow. D'Esperey immediately sent an officer to Lanrezac to point out to him the excellent chance that had arisen.

Now, for the first time, General Lanrezac's fatal weakness was exposed. It is possible to put forward telling arguments in favour of his earlier reluctance to attack the enemy with his whole Army, despite the disingenuousness of his reports and undertakings. But this was something different. This was a local, tactical counter-offensive that was being proposed—an action which, despite its small scale, might have had the most brilliant cumulative effect on the operations both of the 5th Army and of its neighbours. Given the character of von Bülow, who showed considerable nervousness during the day over much less dangerous predicaments, it is easy to imagine what would have been the effect on him of a heavy defeat to the crack Corps of the German Army. Since von Kluck was, at this period, acting under the orders of von Bülow, the results would almost certainly have been felt all the way along the German right wing. But it was not to be. Despite repeated, and at times out-spoken, pleas from d'Esperey all through the morning, Lanrezac refused to give his permission for the attack to take place, and the opportunity passed away.

It is hard to think of a day of war when action on such a huge and momentous scale was conducted in such a fog of uncertainty and misconception. Von Kluck and von Bülow were fumbling and blundering in a manner that reflected the lack of grip and lack of knowledge of the German Supreme Command. Sir John French was making no attempt to control his battle. General Lanrezac was throwing up chances that no one has the right to expect ever to be repeated in war. At G.Q.G., General Joffre was trying to unravel the meaning of a mass of unpalatable facts—a task made all the more difficult by a disinclination to appreciate just what those facts were. Some of the communications that he issued on this day reveal the complete muddle of thought at G.Q.G.

Early in the morning he informed Lanrezac that the 4th French Army "has been engaged since yesterday morning under good con-ditions". He also reported to the Minister of War: "In the main the strategic manœuvre is now completed. Its object and its result have been to place the greater part of our forces at the point where the enemy would be most vulnerable, and to ensure our having at this point *numerical superiority*.* Everything is now in the hands of the troops and their commanders, upon whom it is incumbent to take advantage of this superiority." He was still convinced that "the

* NOTE: Author's italics.

enemy whose columns we are attacking whilst they are marching westward, must be in a difficult situation". And yet, as he wrote these strange words, he was aware that all was far from well with his central Armies, the 3rd and 4th, in the Ardennes. General De Langle de Cary had already reported to him on the previous day's fighting: "All Corps engaged today. General result unsatisfactory. Serious checks . . . [in the direction of Tintigny and Ochamps]. Success gained . . . cannot be maintained. . . . I am sending a fuller report by an officer in a car." The fuller report, when it arrived, filled in a black picture of "disorderly" retreat by the XVII Corps, and "disorganisation" in the Colonial Corps. Joffre could not make it out at all. With commendable frankness, he revealed afterwards, in his Memoirs, how totally mistaken he was at this time about the dispositions and strength of his enemy. G.Q.G. had assessed the strength of the German Fourth Army, facing de Langle de Cary's Army of the same numeral, at six infantry and one cavalry divisions, against De Langle's twelve infantry divisions with two cavalry divisions and two Reserve divisions. The truth was the German Fourth Army, under Duke Albrecht of Wurttemburg, had ten divisions in line, while their Fifth Army, under the German Crown Prince, facing the six active divisions and three Reserve divisions of the French 3rd Army, disposed of another ten divisions, with two cavalry divisions in support. And neither of these German Armies was, as Joffre supposed, marching westwards; on the contrary, they were violently attacking the French directly in front of them.

Under this complete misapprehension, Joffre could only suppose that the failure of the 4th Army and the apparent breakdown of some of its units must be due to "grave shortcomings on the part of their commanders. . . . I asked General de Langle to report to me immediately the names of those officers who ought to be relieved from their command. . . ." That there was dead wood in the French Higher Command was undeniable; equally undeniable that it was most unfortunate to have to cut it out in the midst of battle, and that G.Q.G. itself might have saved several officers' reputations by not setting them impossible tasks. For the time being, however, all that Joffre could do, until he received more and better information, was to order de Langle to resume his offensive. All through the day he remained ignorant of the course of events on his left flank. He did not know that the Belgian 4th Division had abandoned Namur at mid-day; he did not know that the B.E.F. had been engaged in a full-scale battle since 6 a.m.; he did not learn until late that evening that the 5th Army had been in grave danger again, and had continued its retreat. But the impression of growing menace on the left strengthened in him, and began to draw him towards the last-minute re-appraisal which alone could save the Allied Armies.

By noon, a new situation had arisen on the right of General Smith-Dorrien's corps. The German IX Corps resumed its attacks against the Mons salient in full strength, part of its 17th Division advancing towards the flank of the 8th Brigade, the Gordons and Royal Scots, well concealed on the high ground south-east of the town. This attack was beaten back in the same manner as previous ones, but the enemy were now over the Canal in force, and able to envelop the 4th Middlesex, whose position became critical. The Royal Irish were ordered up to support them, but under the heavy fire of the German batteries, both to the east and the north, the battalion had the greatest difficulty in reaching the Middlesex. The British artillery was almost helpless in this sector, because of the enclosed nature of the ground and the impossibility of finding suitable battery positions. The machine guns of the Royal Irish had a small success in dispersing an attempted attack by German cavalry on the right of the Middlesex, but shortly afterwards the German guns found their range and wiped out every man of the machine-gun section. By 3.15 it was clear that both battalions would have to come out of the salient, and they began the hazardous operation of withdrawing in full view of, and in close proximity to, the enemy. Fortunately, the Gordons on their right were in an excellent position to discourage the Germans from any attempt to cut in behind the scattered, weakened fragments of Middlesex and Irishmen.

The Royal Fusiliers had already begun their withdrawal. Their defence of the Mons bridges had been most determined, and won for the regiment two Victoria Crosses. Lieutenant M. J. Dease, in command of the machine-gun section, was awarded one of these posthumously, for he died of his wounds. Private S. F. Godley, also of the machine-gun section, was luckier, for he was able to recount his adventures in a B.B.C. programme forty years later. "During the time I was on the bridge before the actual action started," said Godley, "a little boy and girl came up on the bridge, and brought me some rolls and coffee. I was thoroughly enjoying the rolls and coffee, and talking to the children the best I could, and the Germans started shelling. So I said to this little boy and girl: 'You'd better sling your 'ooks now, otherwise you may get hurt.' Well, they packed their basket up and left."

"The Germans came over in mass formation and we opened fire. . . . During the action we lost Lieut. Maurice Dease . . . and I came under the command of Lieut. Steele. . . . We carried on until towards evening when the order was given for the line to retire. I was then asked by Lieut. Steele to remain and hold the position while the retirement took place, which I did do, although I was very badly wounded several times, but I managed to carry on. I was on my own at the latter end of the action. Of course, Lieut. Dease lay dead by the side of me, and Lieut. Steele, he retired with his platoon. I remained on the bridge and held the position, but when it was time for me to get away I smashed the machine gun up, threw it in the Canal, and then crawled back on to the main road, where I was picked up by two Belgian civilians, and was then taken to hospital in Mons. . . . I was being attended to by the doctors in hospital, having my wounds dressed, when the Germans came in and took the hospital. I was asked a good many questions. What regiment did I belong to? Who was my Commanding Officer? But I knew nothing."

As the Royal Fusiliers fell slowly back, covered by Private Godley at his machine gun, the whole British line to the left of them also began its withdrawal. This must not be imagined as a regular, universal movement. Because of the scattered dispositions of the troops on the broken ground of this peculiar battlefield, and also, to a certain extent, because of the traditional reluctance of the British infantryman to retire when he cannot see any very obvious reason for it, the move was carried out piecemeal, company by company, platoon by platoon, each in its own time, and with varying fortunes. Two companies of Scots Fusiliers found themselves in difficulties among the slagheaps round Frameries. The forward companies of the Northumberlands, who were covering an attempt by the Royal

Engineers to blow up the bridge at Mariette, did not leave the Canal line until 5 o'clock. Captain T. Wright, R.E., won the Victoria Cross here for his gallant persistence in trying to destroy this bridge, although seriously wounded. Lance-Corporal G. A. Jarvis, R.E., also received the V.C. for blowing the bridge at Jemappes after working for one and a half hours on the charges under heavy fire. All along the Canal, the blowing of the bridges was the signal for the infantry to go back to the shorter rear position which General Smith-Dorrien had marked out earlier in the day. The Germans, after the rough treatment they had already received, were understandably slow in following up these determined men; some of the West Kents, for example, were still in their original positions, north of the Canal, at dusk. On the extreme left, the Cornwalls were undisturbed until 4.45 p.m., when they dispersed a mass of cavalry, coming down the road from Ville Pommeroeul. The 19th Brigade was not attacked until 5 p.m.; this marked the arrival of the German IV Corps, which might have been on the field two hours earlier, but for the time von Kluck had wasted, the previous day, under the impression that the B.E.F. was at Tournai. The two divisions of this Corps could have produced a serious result if they had been present in time to co-ordinate their attack with that of the III and IX Corps. As it was, they effected nothing.

However, it was too much to expect that Smith-Dorrien's corps would be able to get away without having to pay the price somewhere. The situation in the salient remained confused, with the Germans filtering now through Mons itself into the back areas of the 8th Brigade. The 4th Middlesex were in considerable trouble, some of their rear parties being overwhelmed in rifle pits which they took over from the Royal Irish; the machine-gun section, which had done splendid work throughout the day, was captured in the end, having fired off its last rounds, with the water boiling in the jackets, into the enemy who were closing in on it. Finally, the remnants of the battalion, much scattered, fell back through the Royal Irish. This regiment, in turn, began to withdraw again, but found the Germans behind it; it was forced to make an awkward detour over the high ground of the Bois la Haut, where the Gordons were still in position, covering the right flank of II Corps.

The last important German attack of the day was delivered against this part of the front. It came at a critical time. The 23rd Battery, Royal Field Artillery, which had been posted on the summit of the ridge, was coming away from it down one of the lanes behind, when it was ambushed by some of the enemy who had advanced through Mons. The Germans fired from behind a barricade, and shot down the leading teams and drivers of the battery at short range. The gunners, helped by an escort of Gordons, at once attacked the barricade, and drove the Germans from it. But it was alarming to have this sort of thing going on in the rear, while a heavy assault developed in front. Fortunately this flank position was as strong and suited to defence, with a smooth, open glacis before it giving a fine field of fire, as the rest of the line had been difficult. The Gordons and Royal Scots, supported by two companies of Irish Rifles, broke up this attack with no more trouble than they had experienced over earlier ones. German casualties were very heavy; the 75th Regiment alone lost 5 officers and 376 men in this attempt to pin down the 8th Brigade. Its failure persuaded the German commanders that it would be as well to let the British go, if they wanted to, and apart from some patrol skirmishes, this was the end of the day's fighting. Soon afterwards the British were amazed to hear the German bugles blowing the 'Cease Fire' all the way down their line. Not merely in tactics, but in some of their conventions, the Germans were still as far from grasping the new nature of war as the Allies.

And now it was a matter, from dusk until the early hours of the next morning, of extracting the last outposts and rearguards, and forming the II Corps on its second position. This was anything but easy. As the two divisions withdrew, a dangerous gap of some 2 miles occurred between them. The Germans, fortunately, were in no condition to take advantage of this. Some of their units, indeed, were so shaken that they even feared a British attack on them. The Colonel of the Brandenburg Grenadiers told his officers: ". . . if the English have the slightest suspicion of our condition, and counter-attack, they will simply run over us". Nevertheless, the gap was alarming; fortunately, it had been foreseen by II Corps H.Q., and three battalions had been borrowed from I Corps to cover it. As it turned out, the I Corps units were not needed, and returned to their Corps next day. Meanwhile, on the right, Brigadier-General Doran delicately extricated the 8th Brigade and its supporting artillery. The 23rd Battery cleared the lane, and quietly got all its guns away; the 6th Battery manhandled its guns down the slopes, and then hooked them in. The Gordons marched off at midnight, and then the Royal Scots. The whole brigade was in its second position, tired but unbroken, by 3 a.m.

It was hard to form immediately any accurate impression of the results of the day. Despite the unfamiliar quality of modern war, the shattering noise, the smoke, the concussion, the sense of annihilation under heavy bombardment, the general feeling in II Corps was that it had done pretty well. As we have seen, there was a tendency to believe that casualties had been much higher than they in fact were. But in the units which had been in actual contact with the enemy, this was offset by a clear view of the enemy's losses in their suicidal mass attacks. The sense of being opposed by great numbers, which might have been discouraging, was also offset by the realisation that these had been brought to a standstill by the deadly British musketry. The worst aspect of this preliminary assessment was the dispersal of units; parties of men came in all through the night; some were still coming in next day; some only rejoined their regiments much later. This helped to create the impression of severe loss where it did not exist. The actual casualties of the B.E.F., as finally estimated, were just over 1,600 of all ranks, killed, wounded and missing, and two guns had to be abandoned. Almost half of these casualties were sustained by two battalions: the 4th Middlesex, with over 400, and the 2nd Royal Irish, with over 300. The Middlesex had gone into action with about 1,000 men. At the roll-call that night, the battalion numbered 275. The difference between the apparent and the real loss is accounted for by men coming in long after the fight was over; but it signified all the difference between a shattered battalion, and one that had suffered severely and yet remained unbroken. This same battalion was able to give a good account of itself again, only three days later, at Le Cateau. The distribution of casualties did, however, mean a considerable weakening of II Corps, and in particular of the 3rd Division. It is important to remember this, in view of subsequent events. In the I Corps, the total casualties of the day amounted to 40, and in the Cavalry Division even fewer. The private diary of an officer of the Scots Guards (I Corps) speaks of August 23rd as "a day of rest", while the battalion diary makes no mention of the battle that was raging only a few miles to the north. Mons was entirely a II Corps battle, and the fact that it ended in a withdrawal takes nothing from the achievement of Smith-Dorrien's two divisions, who were faced by never less than four, and finally by six German divisions. The German losses have never been fully computed, but must have been severe. A German monograph on the battle admitted: "Well entrenched and completely hidden, the enemy opened a murderous fire . . . the casualties increased . . . the rushes became shorter, and finally the whole advance stopped . . . with bloody losses the attack gradually came to an end." The complete failure of the Germans to push home what costly advantage they had won confirms this picture. It did not, however, prevent their propagandists from building fantasies. The diary of an officer of the First Army records, the following day: "We hear that the British cavalry has been annihilated, and that six English divisions have been exterminated as they were detraining." The men who had actually met the B.E.F. knew better, and treated it with marked respect when they advanced against it again.

Nevertheless, the hard military fact remains, that this was a battle that should never have been fought at all. Its only durable results were the distrust of the French that was born on this day, and the conviction of the British infantry that, man for man, they were superior to their enemies.

As the brigades of II Corps took up their new positions, 2 to 3 miles south of the Canal, and along a line which was only a little more than half as long as the one they had defended, it was with no other thought in mind than that they would be resuming action on this line, and shortly have to defend themselves resolutely again. It was not until 11 o'clock that night that a message from G.H.Q., summoning his Chief Staff Officer to receive new orders, indicated to Smith-Dorrien that all might not be well, and it was not until 3 a.m. on the 24th, when this officer returned, that he learned that his position was untenable.

It had taken G.H.Q. a long time to arrive at this conclusion, and, stubborn to the last, they had refused to accept it until it was thrust on them by Joffre himself. Henry Wilson's diary entry is perfectly frank:

"During the afternoon I made a careful calculation, and I came to the conclusion that we only had one corps and one cavalry division (possibly two corps) opposite to us. I persuaded Murray and Sir John that this was so, with result that I was allowed to draft orders for an attack tomorrow by cavalry division, 19th Bgde., and IInd Corps, to N.E., pivoted on Mons, Just as these were completed (8 p.m.) a wire came from Joffre to say we had 2½ corps opposite us. This stopped our attack, and at 11 p.m. news came that the Fifth Army was falling back still farther. Between 11 p.m. and 3 a.m. we drafted orders and made arrangements for retirement to the line Maubeuge—Valenciennes. It has been a day of sharp fighting and severe disappointment. If the Cabinet had sent six divisions instead of four, this retreat would have been an advance and defeat would have been a victory."

It is difficult to imagine a more ridiculous summary than this, by a man in a responsible position. There is only one statement in it that stands inspection: the reference to the 5th Army. To begin with, there is the "careful calculation"; we have seen that two enemy Corps and a cavalry division were identified by their casualties and prisoners at the very beginning of the day. Then there is the revelation that Wilson persuaded Murray and French to accept his views; considering what they had already been told more than once by Spears and their own Intelligence Section, this says little for their judgment. After that, there is Wilson's plan of attack—excellently contrived to place the left wing of the B.E.F. well inside the jaws of the German envelopment. Nor does Joffre's information, useful as it proved in putting a stop to these follies, bear much relation to the truth; there were already three Corps opposite the B.E.F. with another coming down fast on their left wing. As to "drafting orders and making arrangements for retirement", it would appear from other sources that these were less to Wilson's taste than planning impossible offensives. General Smith-Dorrien tells us that when his Chief-of-Staff returned from Le Cateau, "I naturally asked him for the plan of retirement, and was told that G.H.Q. were issuing none, though he had gathered that the idea was for the I Corps to cover the retirement of the II, but that I was to see Haig and arrange a plan with him." This is confirmed by the Official History: ". . . the actual order of retirement to be settled by the two Corps commanders in consultation". Smith-Dorrien grimly remarks: "There must have been some very good reason why four or five hours of valuable time had been lost by sending for Staff Officers instead of sending the order and plan for retirement directly the Chief had decided on it." The only good reason would seem to be that the Operations Branch of G.H.Q. had, to a large extent, lost its head; fortunately, other branches were not similarly affected. Finally, Wilson's last point: it is at this stage that one feels gratitude to Kitchener, whatever his motives had been, however apparently illogical, for with-holding the extra two divisions of the B.E.F. at the beginning. One of them was, in fact, in the process of moving to the battle area; its presence alone, never mind that of two divisions, might easily have impelled G.H.Q. into further rashness, which might have smashed up the whole Army.

However, incomplete as it was, Joffre's information served its purpose. Its main source was the 5th Army, where, once again, all was far from well. The relative quiet of the morning had given way to a bad afternoon. The III and X Corps were attacked again, and again gave ground. Both Corps were very much shaken. And this time the flanking Corps of Lanrezac's Army were also drawn in. On his right von Hausen's Saxons resumed their attack along the line of the Meuse, while on his left the French lost the last bridges over the Sambre. Strangely enough, due to the fumbling and timidity of the two German Army Commanders, von Bülow and von Hausen, these two attacks, instead of assisting each other, tended to nullify their respective results. The best direction for von Hausen's attack was south-west, towards Givet, for this would have brought him across Lanrezac's line of retreat. Von Bülow, however, was anxious about his left flank, and asked Hausen to advance westwards instead, to bring direct help to the Second Army. Then, as von Bülow's own attacks seemed to be going well, he cancelled this request; von Hausen prepared once more to throw his weight south-westwards. But the French XVIII Corps reacted sharply to its early setbacks, and counter-attacked sufficiently firmly to re-establish its position, though it could not win back the Sambre bridges. Von Bülow became alarmed at once, and again appealed to von Hausen for help. By the time it was realised that the French counter-offensive was merely local, and had, in any case, been stopped, it was too late for von Hausen to make any useful progress around Givet. He had been placed in an invidious and difficult position; but one cannot help thinking that a little more determination and purpose in developing his own plans might have saved him much worry and brought him more reward.

Whatever the faults of German generalship may have been on the 23rd, the overall result of their manœuvres was success. All along the centre and right of their great line of battle, their troops had won ground; the Fourth and Fifth Armies were advancing in the Ardennes; the Second and Third Armies were driving Lanrezac further back again; the First Army had had a bad time, but it had made the B.E.F. withdraw. Lanrezac's habitual pessimism was much increased by the new threats that had arisen on the flanks of his Army. About 9 p.m. he decided to retire again, and as he seemed to be making no arrangements for letting Sir John French know of this decision, Spears had to make another journey to Le Cateau to inform him of it. By the time he got there, of course, Joffre's message had already arrived, and all question of a British offensive on the 24th was ruled out. But it was Spears' information about events on the 5th Army front, and Lanrezac's new retreat, that brought about French's decision to withdraw his own Army. It also confirmed French's now rapidly-developing distrust of his neighbour on the right, who had seemed quite content to leave the British in the lurch, while his own 5th Army retired to safety. These were bad moments, fraught with ugly incidents and a growing awareness of very frightening facts. The British Army was saved by the skin of its teeth, more, perhaps by the efforts of Spears, a subaltern, than by any other single man.

Along the front, the exhausted soldiers were trying to snatch a few hours' sleep after their exertions of the day. At the headquarters of the two Army Corps and the divisions, Staff Officers were working feverishly on the details of the retirement which, it was now seen, could not start too soon. The wounded were being evacuated, as far as possible; the dead lay upon the field. The Battle of Mons was over. The Great Retreat was about to begin.

Part Two : Retreat

6

The Retreat Begins

WHEN AN ARMY IS COMPELLED suddenly to retreat, with the enemy close upon its heels, the problem of feeding and supplying it becomes stupendous. If supplies are held too far forward, it is at the risk that they will fall into the enemy's hands; if they are kept too far back, lack of food, medicine or ammunition may be added to all the other stresses afflicting the troops. The burden of responsibility on the Quartermaster-General's Department—never light—becomes intense. We have seen that the Quartermaster-General of the B.E.F., Major-General Sir William Robertson, was a realist who had recognised, early in the campaign, the need to be prepared for more than one contingency. While Henry Wilson and the Operations Section were still living in their dream world, Robertson, on the day *before* the Battle of Mons, was already taking steps to prepare for a possible change of base, should things go wrong. His grim pre-occupations served the Army well, for immediately it became clear that the axis of the B.E.F.'s retirement could not be along the line of its advance.

The two features which were to dominate the entire Retreat of the British Army from Mons came into play from its very beginning. These were the German obsession with envelopment, demonstrated in von Kluck's persistent pressure round the left wing of the B.E.F., and the blindness that often accompanies obsession, revealed in the German commander's entire failure to keep track of the B.E.F.'s actual movements, or anticipate them. As soon as he had driven the B.E.F. off the Canal line, he convinced himself that the British would retire westwards, towards the Channel ports; accordingly, he sent off the whole of the II Cavalry Corps, three divisions strong, under von der Marwitz, to head them off from this direction, and moved his four infantry Corps with the intention of driving the British Army into the fortress of Maubeuge, which lay behind its right flank.

There was a brief period during which von Kluck's suppositions might have proved correct. Spears had remained at G.H.Q. on the night of the 23rd, and returned to Lanrezac's headquarters the next morning, carrying with him Sir John French's decision as to the line on which his Army would retire. This decision was so important, and worried Spears so much, that he wrote down what was said to him: "I was to make it quite clear to General Lanrezac that should the left flank of the British Army be seriously threatened, the Commander-in-Chief intended to retire on his lines of communication, in which case General Lanrezac must look after his own left flank, as the British would no longer hold themselves responsible for covering it." Once again, French's volatile temperament seems to have got the better of him. The note of pique is clearly perceptible in this message. French was now in the full grip of resentment at the manner in which Lanrezac had treated him; the sense of having been 'let down' became a guiding force in him for the greater part of the Retreat. At the same time the unreality of ideas at G.H.Q. is to be seen in the sheer impracticability of the course of action proposed. There was no question of retreating westward *if* his left flank was seriously threatened; it was the very seriousness of this threat that forced him to continue southward, to disengage his Army.

Lanrezac, to his credit, did not fume at Spears when he received French's message. Perhaps he thought that this sort of behaviour was only what one might expect from such 'amateur' soldiers as the British. He accepted the information, and passed it on at once to Joffre. Needless to say, the idea of the B.E.F. withdrawing towards Amiens, while the French fell back to cover Paris, opened up fearful prospects, for Joffre, of German forces pouring through the gap thus created, and destroying the Allies in detail. In 1918 a similar crisis almost won the War for Germany, and brought about the long-contested appointment of an Allied Supreme Commander. Joffre enjoyed no such authority. "What preoccupied me the most," he wrote later, "was the encircling movement which the Germans appeared to be developing on our left. Now, it was the British alone who could offset this menace, and yet it was precisely this army to which I had no right to give orders. I had to content myself with suggesting to Sir John French that . . . if the presence of superior forces should oblige him to fall back, he might do so in the general direction of Cambrai." This at least would preserve some contact between the Allies; but Joffre's uneasiness drew his thoughts on further, to the germ of the idea which saved the Allied cause. At this stage it took a very simple form: "It seemed to me necessary above all to place on the left of the British Army French troops to which I had the right to give orders." Out of this instinct of self-preservation came the re-grouping of the French Armies which alone could check the German advance.

Fortunately, the instinct of self-preservation began to work in Sir John French also. Fortunately too, the impression that Joffre had made on him at their interview was as warm and reassuring as Lanrezac's had been bad. He responded quickly to Joffre's suggestion, and replied to him at 3 o'clock: "I am falling back slowly to position Maubeuge, Valenciennes. . . . If driven from these positions I will act in accordance with your wishes." Reason had supervened; nothing more was heard about retiring to Amiens. There was, however, another alternative which was equally dangerous, and in some ways, French admitted, more tempting. "The fortress of Maubeuge lay close on my right rear. It was well fortified and provisioned. It is impossible for anyone, who has not been situated as I was, to realise the terrible temptation which such a place offers to an army seeking shelter against overpowering odds."

French debated urgently with himself about Maubeuge. But finally two considerations, born of his experience and his military education, forced themselves upon him: "In the first place, I had an instinctive feeling that this was exactly what the enemy was trying to make me do; and, in the second place, I had the example of Bazaine and Metz in 1870 present in my mind, and the words of Sir Edward Hamley's able comment upon the decision of the French Marshal came upon me with overwhelming force. Hamley described it as, 'The anxiety of the temporising mind which prefers postponement of a crisis to vigorous enterprise.' Of Bazaine he says, 'In clinging to Metz he acted like one who, when the ship is foundering, should lay hold of the anchor.' " This settled the matter, and French made up his mind to avoid the trap of Maubeuge; he served the British Army well in that moment. Spears, to whom he told the story in later years, penetratingly selected two points in it to notice: "The first is that had Hamley chosen an image less vivid to express his meaning, it would probably not have remained engraved in Sir John's memory. The second is that Lieutenant-General Sir Edward Bruce Hamley is to be envied by all his countrymen; it has been the privilege of many to serve their country in their lifetime, but it has been the fortune of few to render a great service after death, to stand invisible yet potent across a road leading to disaster and defeat."

And so the B.E.F.'s line of retreat was decided upon by the generals. In its first stages, it was more immediately affected by what the enemy was doing, and how the soldiers dealt with him.

The action of the day was decided by von Kluck's error. If the British were to be driven into Maubeuge, obviously their right flank would need not to be hustled too much, but every pressure would have to be made against their left. With his II Corps now as far south as Condé, and the IV Corps, which had scarcely been engaged at Mons, well forward, von Kluck saw little reason to doubt that he would be able to pin the B.E.F. down. His attack on its left flank, where Smith-Dorrien's corps was still in process of disentangling itself from the confusion of the previous day's fighting, began before dawn, with a violent artillery bombardment. The British transport, of which there was far too much, because of the intention to advance which had held sway until the afternoon of the 23rd, began to get away at 4 a.m. It was not a moment too soon, for by a quarter past five a general attack was developing along the line of the British II Corps. The I Corps was not molested, despite the evident presence of large bodies of the enemy in front of it; but there was nothing reassuring in this, for it only pointed more clearly at the German intention to envelop the left.

The I Corps began to withdraw its main bodies at 5.30 a.m., and as there was no point in allowing the enemy attack to be pushed home against him, Major-General Hamilton ordered his 3rd Division, still on the right of II Corps, to begin retiring half an hour later. The much-tried 8th Brigade got away easily enough, but the rearguards

of the 7th and 9th Brigades, the 2nd South Lancashires and the 1st
Lincolns were caught by the German advance in the mining villages
of Ciply and Frameries. Both battalions, supported by the 109th
Battery, R.F.A., gave an excellent account of themselves. They were
attacked by a whole German division, the 6th, of III Corps; it was a
grim experience for the regiments of this division. Hauptmann von
Brandis, of the 24th Brandenburg Regiment, wrote: "Our artillery
is to prepare the assault. . . . A continuous stream of gun and
howitzer shell thunders out, hurtling and howling over our heads,
and bursting in dust and smoke on the edge of the village (Frameries).
No human beings could possibly live there. At 7 a.m. six companies
of the regiment advance to the attack. We remain impatiently in
reserve. . . . If we thought that the English had been shelled
enough to be storm-ripe, we were fairly mistaken. They met us with
well-aimed fire." Von Brandis' company then went forward to
reinforce the first attack, the men shouting "*Vorwarts*", and expecting the firing-line to rise and go forward with them, but . . . "There
were only dead and wounded to be seen. Tommy seems to have
waited for the moment of the assault. He had carefully studied our
training manuals, and suddenly, when we were well in the open, he
turned his machine guns on." The 'machine guns', of course, were
mainly the rapid rifle-fire of the 1st Lincolns; but the 109th Battery
also found some excellent targets for shrapnel as the Germans broke
cover. The assault failed, and the German bombardment was
resumed. When, at last, the Germans did enter Frameries, it was to
find that the British had gone. Von Brandis could not with-hold a
soldierly admiration for this model rearguard action: "Up to all the
tricks of the trade from their experience of small wars, the English
veterans brilliantly understood how to slip off at the last moment."
German casualties in the attempt to storm these villages and catch
the 3rd Division were very high. In von Brandis' regiment, "Our
battalion alone lost three company commanders, and, besides every
second officer and every third man," Captain Liebenow of the 64th
Infantry Regiment, stated that his battalion lost "the adjutant, every
fourth man and, of three companies, every lieutenant". Captain
Heubner, of the 20th Infantry Regiment, said: "many of our companies had heavy losses. . . . As on the previous day, the English
again vanished without leaving a trace." Unfortunately, the South

Lancashires, holding on to their positions after the Lincolns had slipped away from Frameries, were caught in enfilade by machine guns as they withdrew past the slag-heaps around that village, and then lost between two and three hundred men. This was the only incident that marred the extraction of the 3rd Division from what might have been a very tight corner. For the rest of the day, the Germans showed no eagerness to come to grips with General Hamilton's tough Regulars.

The 5th Division did not get off so easily. This division had not been in any particular difficulty on the 23rd, when its total losses amounted to less than 400 of all ranks; but now, as von Kluck's attempt to envelop the British left gained momentum, Sir Charles Fergusson found himself contending with no less than three German divisions—one from III Corps, and the whole of IV Corps, which had scarcely been engaged on the previous day. It was as well that von Kluck's miscalculation had caused the German cavalry to wander off to the west on a wild goose chase; their presence would, by all the rules of war, have sealed the fate of Sir Charles Fergusson's division.

The German artillery opened up against the 5th Division before dawn, and very shortly afterwards the infantry came forward. As the heads of the German columns began to emerge on the south side of the mining villages, whose confused labyrinth ran across the whole length of the divisional front, they met with exactly the same sort of reception as the 3rd Division had provided further to the east. At the exits of Hornu they were repeatedly checked by the rapid rifle-fire of the Dorsets and the good shooting of the 37th Battery, R.F.A. The Brandenburg Grenadiers, who had lost so severely the previous day, were brought up again to reinforce the attack. It is an indication of their moral condition, and the effect that the B.E.F. had produced at Mons, that when Hauptmann Bloem, having sent out a scout, learned that the British were retiring, he exclaimed: "What? What do you say? The enemy is retiring? You mean he is advancing." But Sir Charles Fergusson had no intention of allowing himself to be caught, and as the troops of the 3rd Division on his right began to slip back, he gave orders for his own 13th and 14th Brigades to do likewise. There were several untoward incidents. When Frameries was evacuated, a part of the German 20th Infantry Regiment was able to infiltrate behind the British line, and ambushed the first-line transport of the Dorsets as it retired from the front. The Germans appear to have lost most of their dash and enterprise, for the transport escaped, nevertheless. Later, however, the 2nd Duke of Wellington's and a battery of the XXVII Brigade, R.F.A, suffered heavy losses through one of those accidents which were now about to multiply themselves, and cost the B.E.F. dearly. Orders to withdraw failed to reach this battalion. As a result, the Germans were able to work up close to it with guns and infantry. The British battery was only saved by the accurate marksmanship of the Duke's, and for an hour and a half there was sharp fighting, with every possibility of a minor disaster. But when the Germans finally came forward in dense masses to deliver what should have been the *coup-de-grâce*, both the Duke's and the battery rose to the occasion with a salute that stopped the enemy in his tracks. In the lull that followed this, the British units were able to break off the action. The Duke's had suffered nearly 400 casualties, but they had held at bay a whole German brigade of six battalions.

If Sir Charles Fergusson was entitled to a feeling of relief at the extraction of his 13th and 14th Brigades, there was still plenty to worry him on the extreme left of his division. There, the absence of the German cavalry had produced a curious effect. The British Cavalry Division had gone out to find the Germans in the early hours of the day. Naturally, it failed, because the enemy was moving away from the British front. This led General Allenby to believe that the area was clear of Germans, and he began, accordingly, to pull back the brigades of his division. The 19th Infantry Brigade, which had prolonged Sir Charles Fergusson's line, also withdrew. By 11.30 a.m., this whole body of troops which could have covered the left of the 5th Division, had fallen back behind it, congratulating themselves on the ease with which they had eluded the enemy. But it was just at this point that the German IV Corps, whose left wing had been vainly trying to trap the Duke's, brought its right wing into action against the now exposed flank of the 15th Brigade. Sir Charles Fergusson immediately asked General Allenby for help, and the cavalry began to retrace their steps, the 2nd Cavalry Brigade leading.

The fight that followed contained one of the episodes which, when versions of it became known at home, captured and ran away with the imagination of many writers and journalists who were still seeing the War rather in terms of the Charge of the Light Brigade and the Thin Red Line. This was the 'charge' of the 9th Lancers 'to save the guns'. It was a gallant episode, but not quite like the pictures of it that have been drawn. A more correct view of the whole action of which it formed part, around the village of Elouges, is that it represented the only notable success of the day for the Germans in their unavailing attempt to envelop the left flank of the B.E.F.

As soon as he became aware that an attack was developing on his open flank, Sir Charles Fergusson formed a rearguard, composed of the 1st Norfolks and the 1st Cheshires and the 119th Battery, R.F.A., all under Colonel Ballard of the Norfolks. These troops had no time to entrench, but they found natural cover along some higher ground facing almost due westwards towards Quiévrain. Their right rested on a railway line, their left on the old Roman Road known as the Chausée Brunehaut, running north-westwards from the village of Audregnies to cut the Mons-Valenciennes highway east of Quiévrain. It was not a bad position, considering the suddenness with which it had to be found; at least there was open ground, giving a good field of fire, in front of it. When the German infantry tried to cross this space, both British battalions were able to receive them with doses of the rapid-fire which had brought all other German attacks to a halt, and which was no less effective here. It is difficult, therefore, to see what necessity there was for the impulsive action of the 2nd Cavalry Brigade, as soon as it returned to this area. Probably one should attribute it to the confusion and excitement of the moment, when there was every appearance of the Germans striking a heavy blow against the weakly held extremity of the British line.

Whatever the reasons may have been, as the 9th Lancers and part of the 4th Dragoon Guards appeared on the scene at about 12.30 p.m., General de Lisle, commanding the 2nd Cavalry Brigade, ordered them to attack the Germans advancing from Quiévrain in flank, if necessary by mounted action. British cavalry rarely need urging to dash at the enemy. All through the Peninsular War, the Duke of Wellington complained bitterly of this habit of rushing headlong at the foe. At Waterloo, one of his best brigades was ruined by it. The British cavalry had learned much since then, but old habits die hard, and we seem to see a survival of this one in what followed. The 9th Lancers immediately galloped down the Roman road in column of squadrons, supported by two troops of the 4th Dragoon Guards, while another squadron of that regiment swung away down a lane to their left to seize a house whose commanding position would cover the attack. The Lancers swept down the road at full tilt, spearing a few German scouts as they caught them, until they came to a sugar factory on a rise, and a wire fence running beside it. By this time they were under the fire of nine German batteries, and men and horses were dropping fast. Some dismounted by the factory, but the main body, with hardly a check, when they came to the fence, and saw the impossibility of pushing home their charge, swung away to the right, across the front of the British infantry, and re-formed there. Apart from giving the infantry a few minutes' grace before the German assault fell on them, the charge had effected nothing. The cost was high—the bulk of the cavalry division's 250 casualties of the day are accounted for by the losses of the 9th Lancers and 4th Dragoon Guards—but might have been higher. The shooting of both the German artillery and infantry must have been very bad, to allow any part of this splendid target to escape.

Among the Dragoon Guards who took part in this affair was Major Tom Bridges; for him it marked the beginning of a series of personal adventures which were entirely typical of the Retreat. He dashed forward at the head of his squadron, full, as he says, "of the spirit of the 'arme blanche' ". As soon as they came under fire, his horse was hit, and fell; the whole squadron and the machine-gun section seemed to gallop over him, and he was knocked unconscious by a kick in the face. When he came to, he found himself in a cottage, where one or two R.A.M.C. orderlies were looking after some wounded men; the French owners of the cottage had put up the shutters, for bullets were pattering on the walls. "Stiff and sore," says Bridges, "I got a man to help me on to a chair where I could see through the fanlight over the door. I could scarcely believe my eyes. Marching through the corn in open order and perfect formation, with fixed bayonets gleaming in the sun, were line upon line of grey-green German infantry. The nearest could not have been 200 yards away. This sight galvanised me into action, and the back door being barricaded, I went through the open window like the clown in the pantomime." He found a wounded horse which was just able to support him, crawled on to the animal's back, and off they went at its best pace, which was nothing like fast enough, and Bridges had the unpleasant sensation of being "sole target for a whole German army corps".

The advance which had so nearly captured him was that of the German 8th Division, debouching from Quiévrain to attack the Norfolks and Cheshires on the higher ground. The British infantry stood the enemy off with their usual sangfroid. Bridges and his unfortunate horse reached cover safely, thanks to the bad marksmanship of the Germans; on his way, he noted two British guns "firing away at the advancing German hordes as steadily as if they had been on the range at Okehampton". These guns probably belonged to L Battery, Royal Horse Artillery, which, with D and E Batteries further to the left, was now sweeping the advancing German lines with enfilade fire. Four German batteries concentrated together on L Battery, but failed to silence it. Bridges was sure that these guns must be captured, but they were not, and the Royal Horse Artillery, supported by dismounted cavalry, played a great part in arresting German progress.

The 5th Division was by now drawing clear of the enemy, but matters were becoming more serious for the rearguard. On the left, having been checked in the attempt to advance from Quiévrain, the Germans were now trying to work round further to the south; on the opposite flank, their 7th Division was approaching from the direction of Thulin, in the north. Colonel Ballard's two battalions were therefore in danger of being trapped from both sides. They were under heavy fire from a ring of German batteries, which were evidently preparing the way for another infantry assault. At about this time, Bridges, having shot his wounded horse with some regret, and wondering what to do next, met Captain Francis Grenfell of the 9th Lancers, coming back with some of his men, "with a bleeding hand tied up in a bandana handkerchief and bullet holes through his clothes but very exhilarated. They had just saved some guns from capture on the railway line, for which he was afterwards awarded the V.C." The guns in question were the 119th Battery, R.F.A., which had, indeed, been in grave danger, under the furious fire of three German batteries and a machine gun at close range. Casualties were

high among the gunners, and Major Alexander, the battery commander, who also received the V.C. for his work on this day, had
asked Grenfell to help him haul the guns out of their exposed
position. Lancers and gunners together manhandled the guns of the
battery out of action, and it was able to move away. It was a brave
exploit. Some accounts of it, however, have been sadly over-written.
It is often stated that the 119th Battery had been almost "wiped out";
this is not so. The battery's casualties during the day were 30,
approximately one-fourth of its strength. This was bad enough, but
did not prevent the 119th Battery from putting up another excellent
performance only two days later.

Bridges found that the blow on his face had deprived him of
speech, but he indicated to Grenfell that he would wait where he
was, in the hope of finding another horse. Soon, however, he
observed a wholesale thinning out of British troops, and began to
think that the Germans would catch him again. Just at this moment
a blue and silver Rolls Royce sports model drew up in all its glory,
driven by an officer of cavalry Signals who was collecting stragglers
and having a look round. He was being very cool about it. "He
picked me up and after a dash into the village to assure ourselves that
the Germans were really in possession, we whisked round and
followed the retreat. . . ." It was certainly time to go. The cavalry
were falling back, the 119th Battery had gone, the Norfolks were
coming away from their forward position—and now occurred the
first of the serious misfortunes that befell the B.E.F. during the
Retreat. Three separate messages, ordering them to retire, failed to
reach the Cheshires. Their commanding officer was hit, and the
Germans were coming close to them on three sides. The battalion
dropped back slowly, defending itself every inch of the way, and
doing much damage to the enemy. For three hours they kept up this
hopeless running—or rather, crawling—fight. At last, completely
surrounded, reduced to a mere handful, split up into several parties,
the remains of the Cheshires surrendered.

Apart from this unfortunate event, the day had gone astonishingly
well. The fighting had been much more severe than at Mons; the
dangers were enormously greater. But once again Smith-Dorrien's
Corps had completely frustrated the enemy, and fought off hugely
superior numbers. Its casualties were over 2,000, compared with

1,600 the day before—light enough, considering the circumstances, but the total was beginning to add up to a serious loss of strength in II Corps. Nevertheless, its feat was truly brilliant. The average German advance, during the whole of this long summer's day, had been no more than $3\frac{1}{2}$ miles. Apart from the disaster to the Cheshires, there were no large-scale captures. No guns were lost, no transport abandoned. The delicate operation of passing one division across the line of march of the other had been accomplished, so smoothly that the two divisions saw nothing of each other. The purpose of the move was to extract the hard-hit 3rd Division from what seemed to be the point of chief danger, and at the same time shorten the retreat of the 5th. At the end of the day, however, both divisions were in much the same state of fatigue, and their losses were roughly equal; furthermore, the German threat to the left wing had now made that the danger-point for the time being. The one large advantage that von Kluck reaped from the slowness of his advance during the day was the arrival of his II Corps in line with the rest of his Army, and the approach of the IV Reserve Corps, both marching in a direction which would bring them opposite to, or round the British left.

Once again, the I Corps had had practically no fighting to do. Its rearguard, skilfully handled by Brigadier-General Horne, R.A., had exchanged some shots with the enemy, but was never in any danger of being caught. The total casualties in the Corps during the whole day amounted to 100. Nevertheless, the men of I Corps had had anything but an easy time. It had been a day of intense heat; men who took their shirts off to dig trenches during the pauses in the march found their packs almost unbearable next day. The whole Corps had been involved in long marches, some units almost continuously for three days. One battalion commander recorded, as his troops reached their billets at ten o'clock that night: "We had marched 59 miles in the last 64 hours, beginning the march in the middle of an entirely sleepless night and getting only eight hours altogether during the other two nights. Many men could hardly put one leg before another, yet they all marched in singing. The other battalions of the brigade did not arrive till long after dark, but they also marched in singing." If there was less inclination to sing in II Corps, this was understandable. The men of the 3rd Division were still arriving at their halting-place long after nightfall, "the men stumbling along more like ghosts than living soldiers, unconscious of everything about them, but still moving under the magic impulse of discipline and regimental pride. Marching, they were hardly awake; halted, whether sitting or standing, they were instantly asleep." In the 5th Division there were many who had had neither sleep nor food for twenty-four hours. "And this," remarks the Official History, "it must be borne in mind, was only the beginning of the retreat."

One man slept. Major Bridges, having been taken to a dressing-station, where a splintered cheek-bone and slight concussion were diagnosed, spent the night in the hay-loft of a large farm. The two old ladies who had remained there alone gave him a hot drink before he went to bed. In the night the clatter of horses' hooves down below awoke him. He went to the window, and saw, in the moon-light, four Uhlans, questioning one of the old ladies. "There was nothing to be done about it so I went back to bed and slept till day-light."

Joffre's day was largely spent in self-communing on subjects as alarming as they were distasteful. Early in the morning, he reported to the Minister of War:

> "The fears inspired in me during the last few days concerning the aptitude of our troops for offensive operations in the field have been confirmed by yesterday's events, which have definitely checked our offensive in Belgium. . . . We have made progress at certain points, but our retirement at others has compelled a general retreat. . . .
>
> "One must face the facts. Our army corps, in spite of the numerical superiority which was assured to them, have not shown on the battle-field those offensive qualities which we had hoped for. . . .
>
> "We are therefore compelled to resort to the defensive. . . .
>
> "Our object must be to last out as long as possible, trying to wear the enemy out, and to resume the offensive when the time comes."

It must have been a bitter moment, when Joffre composed this message. Was it to be 1870 all over again? After forty years of pre-paration, forty years of careful morale-building, of mental and physical training designed to exploit the natural ardour of the French soldier to the full, was it once again to be shown that he was simply inferior to the German? Certainly there were some who were reaching that conclusion. General Lanrezac was passing over now to the philosophy which guided his conduct throughout the remainder of his tenure of command, a philosophy which he expressed to Spears in these terms: "our men are not sufficiently trained at present to stand up on equal terms against the Germans. On the other hand our field artillery is far superior to theirs, so our guns must do the work, they must do the fighting." Lanrezac began what was to be an endless quest for ideal artillery positions to fight on.

Joffre, however, was not prepared immediately to accept these assumptions. "From all points of the front," he says, "came reports of mistakes made in handling troops, mistakes which had brought about heavy losses and sometimes reduced to nought the offensive and defensive qualities of the men." He decided that the first need was to do something to correct these mistakes. G.Q.G. accordingly issued a tactical instruction which, badly needed and sensible as it was, has an extraordinarily elementary ring about it. It should not, surely, have been necessary, three weeks *after* the outbreak of war, to make points like these:

> "Whenever it is desired to occupy a *point d'appui* the attack must be prepared by artillery, the infantry must be held back and the assault must only be launched from such distance as will permit the objective to be reached with certainty. . . .
>
> "The infantry appears to ignore the necessity of organising itself for long-drawn-out encounters. The practice has been to throw forward immediately numerous units in dense formation, which become immediately exposed to hostile fire and are decimated, with the result that the offensive is stopped dead, and the infantry is often left at the mercy of a counter-attack. . . .
>
> "It is important that our cavalry divisions should always have infantry detachments to support them and to increase their offensive capacity. Time must be allowed for the horses to eat and sleep. . . .
>
> "Army commanders will once more and in the most emphatic way possible call the attention of the troops under their orders to the *absolute necessity* of insuring complete co-operation between infantry and artillery. . . ."

All this was as sound as it was obvious. "Unfortunately," remarks Joffre, "more than a mere written order was needed to change instantly the mentality of an army; it takes a long time for a new idea fully to penetrate such a mass."

To lend impetus to the new idea, he began a searching scrutiny of the Higher Command: "a large number of our generals had shown that they were not equal to their task. Amongst them were some who in time of peace had enjoyed the most brilliant reputation as professors; there were others who, during map exercises, had displayed a fine comprehension of manœuvre; but now, in the presence of the enemy, these men appeared to be overwhelmed by the burden of their responsibility." We have noted instances of this already. The worst, Lanrezac himself, was not yet apparent to Joffre, but there were cases that appalled him. In the V Corps of the 3rd Army, for instance, one divisional commander, "completely losing control of himself and abandoning all sense of duty towards his men, committed suicide." There was nothing to be done about this man, but Joffre promptly set about a weeding-out of the senior ranks which he had, in any case, intended to perform in 1914, had the outbreak of war not prevented it. Perhaps it was as well that he awaited the test of battle, for among those who were approaching retiring age were Foch and Pétain; many younger men were to prove far less hardy than these two, who rose, before the end of the War, to the heights of Allied Generalissimo and Commander-in-Chief of the French Army respectively.

The Government fully endorsed the steps that Joffre was taking. The Minister of War, M. Messimy, wrote to him as soon as he heard of them:

> "My dear General,
> You have sent back to me Generals B. and G. Placing these men at my disposal is not enough when there has been cowardice, as in the case of General G.
> I request that hereafter you send officers relieved of their command to G.Q.G. by motor-car and there have them court-martialled. I consider that, as in 1793, there are only two punishments, dismissal and death.
> You want to win; to do so, use the most rapid, brutal, energetic and decisive methods. . . ."

Later that same day Messimy, obviously much disturbed, sent a further telegram to Joffre, a communication whose note of passion reveals the depth of the chasm between the spirit of the French Government in 1914 and 1940:

> "I have your report concerning those guilty of weaknesses. For such conduct there is only one punishment: immediate

not only a long one in point of time, but that time was filled with large events.

Both Corps were away early on the 25th. Once again the I Corps was little troubled by the enemy, but this time encountered consider-able difficulties with its Allies. The 1st Division, on the extreme right, found itself sharing a road with the French 53rd Reserve Division, belonging to the 5th Army. The weather was exceedingly hot all day, the troops were still tired, and this crowding caused innumer-able exasperating checks on the march, to try the men further. However, the division reached its billets without any seriously un-toward occurrences, and with only 32 casualties from its actions with German patrols. The 2nd Division saw even less of the enemy, but, unfortunately, just as much of the French. Maroilles, the halting place designated for the 6th Brigade, proved also to be the supply re-filling point for the 53rd and 69th Reserve Divisions, which caused inevitable confusion. Added to that, the tail of General Sordet's Cavalry Corps was still passing across the line of march of the 2nd Division, and they had to share roads with it for part of the way. The 4th (Guards) Brigade nevertheless reached its halt at Landrecies by about 4 p.m.; the 6th Brigade arrived at Maroilles at about 6 p.m., and the 5th Brigade at Noyelles around midnight, having had to act as guard over the Sambre bridges until relieved by the French.

The II Corps once more had the more difficult time. Von Kluck was still at a loss to understand the British movements. For some time he remained under the illusion that he had succeeded in pushing the B.E.F. towards Maubeuge—he was probably misled by the I Corps' eccentric march to the Sambre, in order to cross it just below the fortress. Nevertheless he did now pull in von der Marwitz's Cavalry Corps, whose absence had so spoiled his manœuvres the previous day. Again, he inclined his right wing forward, to bring it round the left flank of the B.E.F., where the 3rd Division was now posted. On this flank, all through the day, the rearguards of the 3rd Division, the 19th Brigade to the left of them, and the Cavalry Division, fought a continuous series of small actions to hold the enemy off. None of them amounted to anything comparable with the fighting of the 24th. There were no long-drawn-out defences of localities, no striking successes against enemy masses, and, fortun-ately, no units cut off. All the same, the 3rd Division sustained over

350 more casualties, and the cavalry over 100. Both these figures would certainly have been larger, but for the effect produced on the enemy the day before.

The worst feature of the day for the II Corps was the congestion of the roads. General Sordet's cavalry were passing right across their line; refugees swarmed everywhere; and the British transport itself was presenting a serious enough problem. At the village of Solesmes there was dreadful confusion for a time; here, soon after noon, "a huge mass of British transport was struggling to pass through by roads which were already seriously congested by a crowd of refugees. These, with every kind of vehicle, from six-horse farm wagons to perambulators, everywhere delayed the marching troops, and made it impossible for motor cars carrying Staff Officers to pass the columns." Everything depended upon the rearguards if a serious calamity was to be avoided. The 7th Brigade, under Brigadier-General McCracken, had a sharp fight here to disengage the cavalry. It was providential that the arrival of the 4th Division later made it possible to allocate fresh and unused troops to cover this position. The main body of the II Corps, drenched by a violent thunderstorm that broke in the early evening, arrived in its positions around Le Cateau by about 7 o'clock, wet, hungry and more weary than ever. Some units, however, did not come in until the next morning. The men of the 4th Division at Solesmes also had a sharp engagement before they were able to fall back to the Le Cateau position, arriving about midnight. All were uneasily aware that the Germans, although they had not pressed for a major battle that day, were unpleasantly close, and in great strength.

At the Supreme Headquarters of both the French and German Armies, decisions of the first importance were taken on August 25th. The pendulum of error took a definite swing across the line of battle; as Joffre shed his delusions, von Moltke became more and more the immersed in his, with results that were to prove fatal to the German cause.

The moral condition of his Army was Joffre's main source of anxiety. "We had started out with a series of failures," he says, "and the French soldier is very impressionable—losing confidence as readily as he acquires enthusiasm, yielding to depression as quickly as he becomes exalted. The question I asked myself was, would he be able to hold out under this terrible strain . . .?" Apart from the ground that had been lost, and the painful disorder of some of the retirements, which had, indeed, descended into panic routs at times, there were other indications that all was not well. Knapsacks, and other personal equipment which had been thrown away, littered the routes along which the French had retired; the disproportionate casualties among regimental officers and N.C.O.s made it the more difficult to check indiscipline and restore the firmness of the troops. All this Joffre knew, but for the time being there was nothing he could do about it, except hope that the appointment of better men to the senior commands, and the application of his latest tactical instruction would work a cure in time.

In the field of strategy, he was able to proceed now from the secure, but comfortless base of the man who has accepted the worst. With the morning of the 25th, he says, "It was manifest that the strategic manœuvre which had been in preparation since the 18th had ended in complete failure." He was still tempted to believe that it was partly the German success in the centre, against his 3rd and 4th Armies—which continued to mystify him—that had enabled them to strike such a heavy blow against his left. But he was now prepared to accept that they might have a substantial overall numerical superiority, which could change the aspect of matters fundamentally. How to counteract it was the problem, and now the seed which had been planted in his mind the previous day, when he had seen the need to build up a French force on the left of the B.E.F., bore fruit.

The idea of transferring troops to the left flank had begun, as we have seen, with the purely negative realisation that he must be able to exercise direct command in that area. Now he began to envisage wielding a mass of manœuvre against the swinging tip of the German advance, and the two notions coalesced. The first question was, where should the mass of manœuvre be assembled, and in which direction should it strike? General Berthelot, his Assistant Chief of Staff, argued for an attack from the left of the 5th Army against the inner flank of the German right wing, with a view not merely to checking it, but, with luck, cutting it off from the main body of their Armies, and destroying it. To clinch his argument,

Berthelot pointed out that it would be much easier and quicker to bring troops from the right wing to this area than to move them further west.

It was a strong argument, but, says Joffre, "this conception of General Berthelot did not satisfy me". Its success would depend, as he saw at once, on the ability of the 5th Army to hold out and cover the assembly of his Reserve. As realistic now as he had been wildly optimistic before, he doubted very much whether the 5th Army could do this; and if it failed, he saw the prospect of the German envelopment still succeeding, and his Reserve being rolled up along with the rest of his line. "My own preference," he says, "inclined more and more towards a wholly different solution, which consisted in creating on the outer wing of the enemy a mass capable, in its turn, of enveloping his marching flank." He looked to Amiens as the point of assembly and base of operations of this new group; the decisive battlefield would then stretch from Amiens to Rheims. All day Joffre brooded upon this concept, and weighed it against the other; then he made up his mind, and told his aide, Major Gamelin, to embody it in an order. Like a good soldier, Berthelot accepted his chief's ruling at once, and did his best to make the plan succeed.

For its success, there were three essential prerequisites. First, the 4th and 5th Armies would have to win time for Joffre by fighting determined delaying actions. Secondly, the British would have to fall back as slowly as possible, resisting tenaciously, to check the momentum of the German swing. His peculiar relationship to the B.E.F. continued to worry Joffre, and he decided that it was high time that he and French met again. He arranged an interview at French's headquarters, now removed to St. Quentin, for the following day, and summoned General Lanrezac to be present at it. Thirdly, of course, if sufficient troops were to be collected to give his manœuvre a chance of real success, all eccentric operations would have to be stopped. As it happened, both his 3rd Army, and the Army of Lorraine to the right of it, had just begun local counterattacks with promising results. Not without regret, for successes of any kind were badly needed by the French at this juncture, Joffre ordered these actions to be broken off. Without delay he set in hand the transfer of divisions from his extreme right, in Alsace, from his centre, and from Paris, to the left wing. This was only the first stage;

the new group had, as yet, no name and no commander. But the moment in which Joffre decided to create it was one of the true turning-points of the War.

It was fortunate for the Allies that von Moltke was not of the same stature as Joffre. From the very commencement of operations the grip of his Supreme Headquarters, 200 miles away at Coblenz, on what was actually taking place in the field, had been tenuous in the extreme. By the 25th he had convinced himself that the three victories won by his Armies in Lorraine, the Ardennes, and on the Sambre were of the first order. A leading Berlin newspaper had carried the headline: "France's Spine Broken"—reflecting the attitude and the communiqués of Supreme Headquarters. Von Moltke came to the conclusion that "the great decisive battle in the West had been fought and decided in Germany's favour. . . ." He could not have made a more disastrous mistake.

The danger of believing what one wishes to believe is more fatal in war than in any other human activity. There is no doubt that von Moltke was only too eager to form this opinion about operations in the West, because in the East matters were far from satisfactory from the German point of view. The campaign in East Prussia had been mishandled; already a change of command had had to be carried out there, and General von Hindenburg was in process of taking charge. The position, however, remained serious. Von Moltke decided, under the impression of "decisive victory" in one theatre, to transfer troops from it to the other. Two Army Corps were accordingly selected to switch from the Western Front to the East. The question was, where should they come from?

> "I intended," says von Moltke, "to take these reinforcements from the Seventh Army, which had made as little progress towards the Moselle as the Sixth. Both these Armies, however, consistently reported that they were opposed by superior numbers of the enemy, also that losses had been so heavy that no units of the Seventh Army were fit for employment elsewhere until they had been brought up to strength again. For these reasons, it was decided to send two corps from the right wing . . . to the Eastern Front."

Von Schlieffen must have turned in his grave. This was the exact opposite of his intention, which had been to bring troops across from the left to the right, as soon as the great swing was well in motion. The German right wing had already been weakened by the detachment of three Corps, two to watch the Belgians in Antwerp, and one more to invest Maubeuge. Now, the two Corps released by the fall of Namur were also to be taken away. "I admit that this was a mistake," said von Moltke afterwards, "and one that was fully paid for on the Marne."

The effects, both of Joffre's return to reason and of von Moltke's error, took time to work themselves out. There would be many a crisis yet, before the peril of the Allied cause was averted. The soldiers of both the French and British Armies, exhausted and ravenous, would have to endure many more depressing marches with their backs to the enemy, their belief in a counter-stroke wearing ever more thin, before the opportunity came for Joffre to put his new plan into effect. But beneath all the harrowing tribulation of the next ten days, the under-current of the war was turning steadily into its new and hopeful channel.

7

Landrecies and Le Cateau

FOR THE B.E.F. and its commander, August 26th was the most alarming day of the Retreat. The troubles, indeed, had begun the night before, stemming chiefly from the separated march of the two Army Corps on either side of the Forest of Mormal. The thick timber of this forest created a blind area on the inner flank of both Corps. In this area the Germans were groping forward with no more certainty about the B.E.F.'s movements than they had displayed before. It had come as a great surprise to von Kluck, on the morning of the 25th, to learn that the British had been seen by one of his aircraft, marching southwards towards Le Cateau—"an almost opposite direction to what was supposed earlier in the morning". On receiving this information, von Kluck ordered his Army to wheel round and head off the B.E.F. towards the east. The skilful withdrawal of the II Corps and the cavalry just pulled them clear of this movement, but it continued, nevertheless. The effect was to draw the advance-guards of the German III and IV Corps southeastwards, across the rear of the II Corps, through the forest (which had good east-west communications, as we have seen) towards the blind flank of the I Corps.

The first alarum occurred at Landrecies, where the 4th (Guards) Brigade had halted, together with the headquarters of the I Corps. At about 5.30 p.m. there was a panic among the refugees, who flocked as thickly down the roads here as along the rest of the B.E.F.'s route. They were streaming into the village, says General Charteris, one of Haig's Staff Officers, "shouting that the Uhlans were hard at their heels, and some of them flourished Uhlan lances and accoutrements to prove their statements. D. H. told me to get on my horse and, with one orderly, to ride back and investigate."

Charteris made a thorough reconnaissance, but could find no sign of any enemy troops in the immediate vicinity. It was a false alarm. Half an hour later, however, there was a more serious incident further to the north, at Maroilles, where the 6th Brigade was just coming into its billets. Patrols of German infantry, belonging to the III Corps, emerged from the forest and drove in the pickets of the 15th Hussars, divisional cavalry of the 2nd Division. The Hussars resisted stubbornly, until the Germans brought up a field gun; they then fell back until they met a company of the 1st Royal Berkshires, coming up in support. A trick which was to become familiar was now played on the British troops. The Germans challenged in French, and lured forward an officer whom they made prisoner. But they could make no further progress. The remainder of the Berkshires came up shortly afterwards, having made their way with much difficulty through the transport and refugee congestion in Maroilles itself. By this time the Germans had retired to the Sambre bridge, which they prepared to defend vigorously. The only approach to it was across a long open causeway, and the attempt of the Berkshires to rush this cost them 60 casualties. As no more German troops put in an appearance, the action then came to an end, but it was a nervous night for the 6th Brigade, expecting a new attack at any moment.

While all this was going on, the Germans were arriving in reality at Landrecies. The first indication of their presence was the sound of wheels and horses approaching through the darkness on the road north-west of the town. According to one German account, this was regimental transport, which had been ordered to precede the troops into Landrecies—so little did they expect to meet any resistance there. A picket of the 3rd Coldstream Guards was stationed on the road, and the sentry challenged. Once again the Germans answered in French. An officer went forward to question them, and they kept up the exchange of French, meanwhile edging closer. Then, suddenly they attempted to rush the picket, and even managed to seize his machine gun and drag it a few yards away. The Coldstream gave them a volley, and recovered the gun; the fight was on.

The disadvantages of a Corps headquarters being mixed up with advanced troops were now seen. In Landrecies itself, as the Germans returned to the attack, and brought up artillery in support of it, there was great confusion, and reports went round that the place was surrounded. General Charteris had been snatching some much-wanted sleep, when he was awakened by the noise. He went off immediately to find Haig. "D.H. ordered the whole town to be organised for defence, barricades to meet across the roads with furniture and anything else handy, all secret papers, etc., to be destroyed. He sent me off to prepare a big school building for defence, giving me a couple of companies of Guards as a working party. For once he was quite jolted out of his usual placidity. He said, 'If we are caught, by God, we'll sell our lives dearly.'" It was not usual for Haig to talk or act like this. He was suffering from some disorder all through the previous day, for which he had been treated with a dose of "what must have been something designed for elephants, for the result was immediate and volcanic!" according to Charteris. It had left him weak and looking ghastly all day.

Charteris himself was not happy about the destruction of documents. There were some which he felt it might be advisable to keep

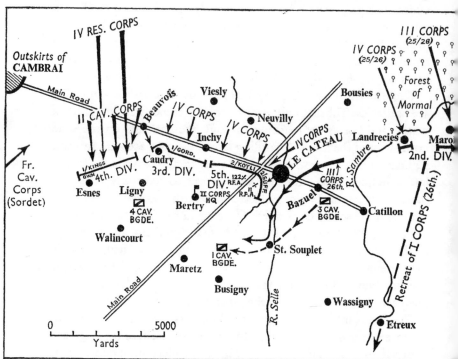

The actions of August 25/26th: Landrecies, Maroilles, the Battle of Le Cateau

in existence as long as possible. He was able to extract these, and put them in his pocket. In the streets, he found some astonishing scenes taking place: "men were throwing mattresses and chairs out of the windows for the barricades, which others were making as best they could. The few inhabitants left were protesting feebly. The Guards had arrested and tied up a French officer who had lost his head, and was making an ass of himself." At the outskirts of the town, the Coldstream were keeping the enemy at bay with all their traditional coolness; behind them, the working parties were displaying the same sangfroid (in marked contrast to the agitation of some Staff Officers), and evidence of the opportunism that rarely deserts the British soldier. "I saw one rather pompous and unpopular Staff Officer walking towards me," says Charteris, "and a man at an upper window taking deliberate aim with one of those great soft French mattresses, and hitting him fair and square with it. Down went the pompous one, buried in the feather mattress, to the immense glee of the men. He was, of course, none the worse for it, but very, very angry."

Not far away another British officer was demonstrating that it was not only the French who could lose their heads and make fools of themselves. Charteris heard a rattle of shots close by, and, on investigating, found a senior officer, in a very excited state, firing his revolver down a street. There was also a military policeman, watching this spectacle with deep interest, so Charteris asked him what was in the street: " 'Nothing, sir,' he said with a smile, 'but some officers' horses.' So I asked him, 'Why the —— don't you stop him?' 'Well you see, sir,' he said, 'he is a full Colonel, and his own horse is there with the others, and besides he's very excited and it may ease him.' So I asked the 'full Colonel' if he would care to come and help me with my job instead of shooting horses, and he quite amicably agreed. So off we went together."

All sorts of legends became current about this fight in the dark at Landrecies. They are important, because they reflect the great mental confusion which was its chief product. Sir John French, for example, in a despatch to Lord Kitchener on the 27th, described the action as follows:

> "A German infantry column, about the strength of a brigade, emerged from the wood north of the town and advanced south in the closest order, filling up the narrow street.

"Two or three of our machine guns were brought to bear on this magnificent target from the other end of the town. The head of the column was checked and stopped, a frightful panic ensued, and it is estimated that, in a very few minutes, no less than 800 to 900 dead and wounded Germans were lying in the streets."

Needless to say, when this became public, the Press made the most of it. The Official History, however, reads a little more coolly. The action was brisk enough, indeed, for several hours. The Germans brought up artillery, and made repeated attempts, by the light of burning buildings, to break through the outpost line of the Coldstream Guards.

"The engagement," says the Official History, "went on until past midnight when a howitzer of the 60th Battery was brought up by hand within close range and with its third round silenced the German guns. This seems to have decided the issue; and the enemy drew off. The losses of the 3/Coldstream were 120, those of the Germans, according to their official casualty lists, were 127. By about 4 a.m. on the 26th, all was quiet again on the line of the I Corps."

Apart from the fact that the Guardsmen of the 4th Brigade behaved as one would expect them to behave, rising readily above the fatigue of the day's march and the first surprise, there would be nothing particular to note about this night action at Landrecies, were it not for the remarkable impression which it made on the minds of commanders. Haig, in particular, was shaken, and the manner in which he passed on his own reaction had far-reaching effects. When Charteris had finished his work at the school building, he returned to find his Corps commander. "The attack had died down a bit, and I found him just on the point of getting into his motor-car to try to get through the enemy line, which must obviously be thin, to join the main body of the Corps. He told me to get in front with the driver and take charge of the car and choose the best route. I asked for five minutes to study the map. Then off we started. It was rather eerie work, quite dark and of course no lights on the car. There was a little mist, which was helpful in one way, but it made it more difficult to find the road. There was still a good deal of firing, and it looked rather a forlorn hope to try to get through. But anyhow it was better than staying in Landrecies and having sooner or later to surrender, which seemed the alternative." With luck and judgment, they got through. "All the same," says Charteris, "it was a close shave; it might have ended in us all—including D.H.—being prisoners!"

It was Haig's firm belief, when he rejoined the main body of his Corps, after all this excitement and the nerve-racking drive through the dark, that the 4th Brigade was as good as lost. He gave orders at once to the 1st Division to set in hand a rescue operation the following morning. He sent Charteris to find the nearest French troops, and ask for their help. At 1.35 a.m. he also reported to G.H.Q., to the effect that the situation was very critical. Later at 3.50 a.m, he asked that the II Corps, now 8 miles away at Le Cateau, should march upon Landrecies to help him. The effect of all this on G.H.Q., which had itself spent the day in transit from Le Cateau to St. Quentin, was startling. Sir John French's letter to Kitchener shows what sort of picture of events was building up in his mind.

There is no doubt that the dominant impression on French, as the day of the 26th dawned, was of grave crisis arising on his right flank. He had seen the heads of columns of the II Corps coming into the Le Cateau position the previous evening, and "though tired indeed, they had not struck me as being worn out troops". The later information, from I Corps H.Q. made a much sharper impact on him than his own views of II Corps. Still thoroughly disconcerted by this information, he caused Colonel Huguet, at 5 a.m., to send off this message to General Lanrezac:

> "The I Corps has been violently attacked during the night in its billets between Le Cateau and Landrecies, and is falling back, *if it can*,* on Guise, to the south; if not, *south-east** in the direction of La Capelle. . . .
> "Tomorrow, 27th, the general retreat will be continued on Péronne.
> "Under these circumstances, Field-Marshal French asks you to come to his aid by sheltering the I Corps until it can rejoin the main body of the British forces."

The effect of this message on 5th Army H.Q. can be imagined. "The morning of the 26th was a nightmare," says Spears, ". . . The British I Corps was pictured streaming back towards the 5th Army

* Author's italics.

area as had the garrison of Namur, while the Germans poured through the gap left by the defeated British." The mention of Péronne, to the south-west, in the same text as the possibility of the I Corps retiring south-east, must have baffled the French Staff Officers. However, for once Lanrezac rose to the occasion, and immediately ordered his left wing to do what it could to disengage the British I Corps. As it turned out, French help was not needed, for, when morning came, the 4th Brigade and the whole of the I Corps was able to resume its retreat quite quietly. It did not, however, cross the Sambre. It continued to march down the eastern bank of that river, cutting across the loop between Landrecies and Oisy. So far from joining the II Corps on the Le Cateau position, it was actually enlarging the gap, already 8 miles wide, between the two corps. It was in this movement that the true danger to the B.E.F. lay. But Sir John French was by now so obsessed with the non-existent peril to the I Corps, that he seems not to have been able to take in the circumstances that had developed on his left.

When the two Army Corps separated, to march on either side of the Forest of Mormal, the intention was that they would rejoin each other as soon as the obstacle had been passed. There was no question of the Le Cateau position being solely occupied by the II Corps. But when the day ended, the I Corps was still 8 miles away from the nearest troops of the II Corps, and, apart from the exhaustion of the men, the conflicts with the enemy made it impossible for them to close the gap during the night. On the contrary, as we have seen, Haig later asked Smith-Dorrien to move towards him. The latter, in accordance with G.H.Q. instructions, had issued orders for his Corps to resume its retreat next day. But as the evening wore on into night, he began to wonder whether this would be practicable. It was not until midnight that the rearguard of the 3rd Division could be accounted for. Of the position of the Cavalry and 4th Divisions, he knew nothing. Later he learned that the three brigades of the 4th Division only assembled on their position between 3.30 and 5.30 a.m. on the 26th.

At 2 a.m. that morning, General Allenby arrived at Smith-Dorrien's H.Q., and the discussion that followed did much to clarify his mind, though nothing to reassure it. Allenby reported that his brigades were much scattered, and his men and horses "pretty well played out. . . . He wanted to know what I was going to do, saying that unless I could move *at once* and get away *in the dark*, the enemy were so close that I should be forced to fight at daylight." Smith-Dorrien then sent for General Hamilton, whose 3rd Division H.Q. was nearby, and asked him whether his troops could move off at once. Hamilton replied emphatically that they could not possibly get away before 9 a.m. Reflecting that the 5th Division, though less tired, were even more scattered, while the 4th Division had last been seen still engaged in rearguard fighting round Solesmes, Smith-Dorrien concluded that to stand his ground and fight might be the lesser of two evils. He turned to Allenby, and asked him whether he would take orders and act as part of II Corps; Allenby said he would. Smith-Dorrien then said: "Very well, gentlemen, we will fight, and I will ask General Snow to act under me as well." There was a sigh of relief in the room. The die was cast.

It was one thing to make the decision; it was another to implement it. Allenby and Hamilton were present, and could immediately begin passing the order down to their troops. Smith-Dorrien himself went to General Fergusson's 5th Division H.Q., to inform that officer. Like the other generals, Fergusson was relieved at the decision to fight. General Snow, at 4th Division H.Q., did not receive the order until 5 a.m. He later wrote to Smith-Dorrien: "When you sent to me the morning of the 26th to ask if I would stand and fight, I ought to have answered: 'I have no other choice, as my troops are already engaged in a battle of encounter, and it must be some hours before I can extricate them.' " The 4th Division, it should be noted, was still far from complete. The divisional cavalry, divisional cyclists, signal company, field ambulances, field companies R.E., train, and divisional ammunition column, and heavy artillery had not yet arrived. The division, in fact, lacked the very essentials for modern war; General Snow's opinion, therefore, carries particular weight, since he, above all, should have been anxious to avoid a battle.

G.H.Q., of course, had to be informed as early as possible about the change of plan. Smith-Dorrien set down a lengthy explanation of what he was proposing to do, and sent it off by car to St. Quentin, where it arrived about 5 a.m. G.H.Q. replied immediately:

"If you can hold your ground the situation appears likely to improve. Fourth Division must co-operate. French troops are taking offensive on right of I Corps. Although you are given a free hand as to method this telegram is not intended to convey the impression that I am not anxious for you to carry out the retirement, and you must make every endeavour to do so."

"This reply," says Smith-Dorrien, "cheered me up, for it showed that the Chief did not altogether disapprove of the decision I had taken, but on the contrary considered it might improve the situation." French's injunctions, in fact, coincided with Smith-Dorrien's own intentions, which were never to fight a long-drawn-out action, but simply to give the enemy "a stopping blow, under cover of which we could retire". And it must be remembered that, when he selected his position, he did so on the assumption that the I Corps would join him on it. When he decided to fight, he was still unaware that they would not be able to carry out this part of G.H.Q.'s instructions.

Some two hours after receiving G.H.Q.'s first answer to his report, Smith-Dorrien was called away from the battle, which was by now in full swing, to answer a telephone call which he understood to be from Sir John French, whom he had been trying to contact personally for some time. In fact, it was Wilson, who told Smith-Dorrien that French wanted him to break off the action as soon as possible. Smith-Dorrien replied that he would try to do so, but might have to wait until dark. "Henry Wilson then asked me what I thought of our chances, and when I replied that I was feeling confident and hopeful of giving the enemy a smashing blow and slipping away before he could recover, he replied, 'Good luck to you; yours is the first cheerful voice I have heard for three days.' With these pleasing words in my ear, which I shall never forget, I returned to my headquarters." Wilson's remark is a sufficient indication of the state of mind that was prevalent at G.H.Q.; there, the whole picture of the situation on the morning of the 26th was distorted. It may perhaps be partly due to the remnants of that mental confusion that Sir John French could write, even years later, in his book: "In more than one of the accounts of the retreat from Mons, it is alleged that some tacit consent at least was given at headquarters at St. Quentin to the decision arrived at by the commander of the II Corps. I owe it to the able and devoted officers of my Staff to say that there is not a semblance of truth in this statement." We shall find even more unjust falsifications in French's account of the Battle of Le Cateau, which was, in truth, not only the most brilliant exploit of the B.E.F. during the Retreat, but one of the most splendid feats of the British Army during the whole of the War. We must remember, however, that these words were written much later, by a man with a grievance, and possibly also with a bad conscience about Smith-Dorrien. At the time, French thought somewhat differently; and it must be remembered, too, that he had plenty on his mind.

Joffre's new plan of campaign was known as "*Instruction Générale No. 2*". When he set off, early on the 26th, to St. Quentin, to meet French and Lanrezac, Joffre's main intention, apart from renewing contact with his Ally, was to discuss the details of this plan. On arriving, however, he found French much engrossed with the practical problems of his Army; while waiting for French to join him, he had conversations with General d'Amade, who commanded the group of Territorial divisions on the left of the B.E.F., and General Lanrezac, who was in no pleasant temper. Earlier that morning he had been seen, amid a group of Staff Officers, publicly abusing both G.Q.G. and the B.E.F. in the most violent language. The scene produced the worst possible impression on the junior French officer who noted it: "discipline, faith in the leadership of the Supreme Command, alike seemed to be going by the board". It was with great difficulty that his Chief of Staff persuaded Lanrezac to go to St. Quentin at all. But Joffre was glad to have the opportunity of speaking to him; he knew that there was friction between Lanrezac and French, and he was uncertain of Lanrezac's general attitude. The latter, however, "told me that he thoroughly understood my intentions, and he raised no objections. . . . When I insisted on the necessity of having his army make frequent counter-attacks . . . he assured me that he expected to resume the offensive as soon as his forces had debouched from the close country round Avesnes, where his artillery could accomplish little. He also stated that his troops were in excellent condition to make an attack." This trick of saying one thing behind Joffre's back, and something quite opposite to his face, was the weakness that is hardest to forgive in Lanrezac. Quite often, if he had only cared to put them forward properly, his ideas were correct; his subterfuges, however, became positively dangerous.

The conference was not a success. When French arrived with Murray, Joffre had two disagreeable surprises. The first arose out of Sir John's general demeanour: "I expected to find the same calm officer whose acquaintance I had made a few days before; but, to my great surprise, the British Commander-in-Chief started out immediately in a rather excited tone. . . ." The burden of French's heated diatribe was that his Army was now being violently attacked in exposed positions, and that this had been its lot ever since the commencement of operations, largely because of the sudden and headlong retirements of the 5th Army. "He accused this Army of having broken off the fight and left him completely isolated." Lanrezac's response was not encouraging; according to French, he "appeared to treat the whole affair as quite normal, and merely incidental to the common exigencies of war. He offered no explanation, and gave no reason for the very unexpected moves he had made. The discussion was apparently distasteful to him. . . ." Joffre's impression of friction between the two men was more than confirmed, and added to his uneasiness: ". . . their mentalities were so wholly different that they seemed quite unable to work together under the hard strain of battle". French gathered, as some consolation, that Joffre "was by no means satisfied with the action and conduct of his subordinate general". But Joffre was by no means satisfied with French, either—and with reason.

His second, and worse surprise came when French had finished, and Lanrezac had made it clear that he did not wish to contribute anything to the discussion. To give the meeting a more constructive turn, he now referred to his new *Instruction Générale*, and the ideas contained in it. He urged on French the need to do everything possible to bring these ideas to fruition. "I saw by his surprise that he was not acquainted with my intentions, and I asked him if he had received a copy of the Instructions of August 25th which I had sent him. He had not yet seen this paper, as it had never left General Murray's hands." This was disconcerting indeed. Joffre went over the contents of his *Instruction*, in the flat, level tones that were habitual with him. He gave the impression of scarcely believing in what he was saying, and certainly it made no positive impact on French, who raised objections at once, and insisted that he must continue his retreat to St. Quentin. Not even Joffre's promise to order the French troops on the left of the B.E.F. to cover its open flank by active co-operation could shift Sir John from this position. And on this negative note, the conference petered out. "When I left British Headquarters in the early afternoon," says Joffre, "I carried away with me a serious impression as to the fragility of our extreme left, and I anxiously asked myself if it could hold out long enough to enable me to effect the new grouping of our forces." Later, when the news of the day's fighting reached him, this question would present itself even more acutely, and there was nothing in the manner of the British Headquarters Staff at St. Quentin to offset the doubts that were now springing up in Joffre's mind about the dependability of the B.E.F.

When every allowance is made for the fact that G.H.Q. had been in transit itself the previous evening, that Murray had been suffering the first of his partial collapses through sheer fatigue, and that the night had been full of alarums, it still seems an appalling thing that the Commander-in-Chief should have been allowed to meet Joffre without even a rough idea of what was contained in the latest *Instruction Générale*. The excuse was that there had not been time to translate it. This was the duty of Henry Wilson's Operations Section; one wonders what more useful work they found to do, considering that more than half the Army was now in the thick of a battle on the initiative of a Corps commander, while the remainder was retreating in a direction not prescribed by G.H.Q.

The Le Cateau position may be described as a tipped-up reversed "L", thus: ⌐; at the apex of the angle is the small town of Le Cateau itself; the short arm of the figure is formed by the valley of the River Selle, running roughly south-north to Le Cateau, before bending away to the north-west; the long arm is formed by the straight highway to Cambrai, 15 miles away, running through the villages of Inchy, Caudry and Beauvois. The three brigades of the 5th Division were crowded in the angle of the "L", with a small detachment on the east side of the town, waiting to link up with the I Corps when it arrived; the 3rd Division held the centre, with the 8th and 9th Brigades on the high ground overlooking the village of Inchy, and the 7th Brigade in Caudry; the 4th Division continued the line, but bending back in a "refused flank" to Esnes. The total length of the front was about 10 miles. The 4th Cavalry brigade was behind the centre, the 1st and part of the now badly scattered 2nd behind the right, while the 3rd was away to the east, also seeking contact with the I Corps. It was not a bad position, as far as it went; but it had been selected under the impression that the I Corps would be there to prolong it eastwards. Their non-arrival created an open flank which naturally proved to be a serious liability.

The morning of August 26th, the anniversary of Crécy, came with a thick mist. Some British units were still withdrawing to their designated positions, and others were at work entrenching, when the German artillery began firing, about 6 a.m., from north-east of Le Cateau, at the troops on the spurs in the angle immediately behind the town. Almost simultaneously, the enemy appeared on the left flank too, from the direction of Cambrai. That town was still held by the French Territorials under General d'Amade. Forming a tenuous link between these troops and the British left was General Sordet's Cavalry Corps, now very worn with its continuous marches, but still able to strike a blow, as it showed when Joffre's orders to co-operate with the British reached it. Once again, von Kluck was marching into a battle with only the most delusive ideas of his enemy's situation. Despite the encounters at Maroilles and Landrecies, he still believed that the British were trying to edge away to the south-west, and that he would catch them on a more or less north-south alignment between Cambrai and the Sambre. He directed his II Corps upon Cambrai; von der Marwitz's Cavalry Corps was to grip and hold the British left until the IV Reserve Corps could come up from its starting point further to the rear; the IV Corps would hold the centre, and the III Corps would swing across to envelop the British right. As von Kluck planned it, the battle would take the classic "Cannae" shape, and end in the total destruction of what von Kluck not only believed to be the whole B.E.F. but a B.E.F. of six divisions. His Army Corps, however, stumbled into the British positions piecemeal, as they had done at Mons, and the battle was over before their full strength could be developed. In passing, it is worth noting that if even only one of the divisions of Haig's Corps had been near the sector assigned to it, a severe blow might have been struck at the exposed flank of the German III Corps, which would have had to march across their front to reach the battlefield.

But a battle is generally the sum of errors, and no side has the monopoly of them.

The infantry of the German 7th Division (IV Corps) filtered into Le Cateau astonishingly quickly. The first indication of their presence was when they succeeded in ambushing the Cornwall Light Infantry and a wing of the East Surreys in the eastern outskirts of the town. This was the detachment which was supposed to link up with the I Corps. It fell back stubbornly on to the high ground south-east of Le Cateau, where it was shortly joined by the 3rd Cavalry Brigade under Brigadier-General Hubert Gough. This small portion of the British force not merely disengaged itself with remarkable success, but was able to later to play a significant part in the action on the right flank.

The threat to that flank developed immediately. The German infantry began to creep through the mist down the valley of the Selle, and at the same time to push out on to the high ground to the east. It became clear that as soon as they could bring batteries into action from this quarter, the 5th Division would be doubly enfiladed. Its own artillery was very exposed, with most of the batteries well forward on the open spurs overlooking Le Cateau. As the Germans extended their attack to the west of the town, and more of their guns came into action on the heights beyond the Cambrai road, the British soon found themselves in grave danger. The 2nd Suffolks of the 14th Brigade, and the 2nd King's Own Yorkshire Light Infantry of the 13th Brigade had to endure a deluge of artillery fire to which they could make no answer at all. The British guns could at least make some reply; on other hand, they presented the German gunners with excellent targets, which they concentrated on immediately.

In this sector, the fight continued with mounting fury for six hours, before the German could make any impression on the 13th and 14th Brigades. The 11th Battery, R.F.A., frequently firing at point-blank range to support the Suffolks, was subjected to dreadful punishment; by 10 o'clock, when the enemy's infantry began to come forward in masses west of Le Cateau, this battery had lost all its officers, and only one gun could still be manned. But that gun remained in action, with the rest of the XV and XXVIII Brigades of the Royal Field Artillery. The 122nd Battery took as its first target a platoon of German infantry in line, shoulder to shoulder, which emerged from a fold in the ground. The battery commander ordered "one round gun fire", and the entire platoon was instantly destroyed. A machine gun of the Yorkshire Light Infantry did excellent work in protecting the left flank of the Suffolks, and that regiment, supported by the 52nd Field Battery, by steady marksmanship, foiled every attempt of the enemy to build up a firing line near enough to the British position for an attack to be pushed home. By 11 o'clock, however, the position was so serious and casualties in the Suffolks so heavy, that the Manchesters, in brigade reserve, were ordered up to support them, together with part of the Argyll and Sutherland Highlanders of the 19th Brigade, Smith-Dorrien's only Corps reserve. All these units had the greatest difficulty even in reaching the Suffolks, through the storm of fire that swept the forward face of the slope which they were so splendidly defending. By noon, their situation was even worse. The last gun of the 11th Battery was silenced; the Germans were increasing in numbers and coming steadily nearer; but there was no thought of giving way.

Along the centre of the British line, against the left of the 13th Brigade and the 3rd Division, there was no serious German pressure before mid-day. There was considerable shelling, particularly on the village of Caudry, held by the 7th Brigade. This brigade was very weak, its units scattered and broken up by their efforts of the previous night. Indeed, one battalion, the 2nd Royal Irish Rifles, had been given up for lost altogether, and only rejoined the brigade, in company with the 41st Battery, R.F.A., at 9 o'clock that morning, when the battle had already been engaged for three hours. It was as well that the Germans did not press their attacks heavily here from the beginning; what advances they did make were easily held by the rifle-fire of the infantry and the good practice of the British guns. Further to the left, however, where the other horn of the envelopment was coming into play, it was a different matter.

On the left flank, as on the right, the action opened with a surprise of the British forces; here, however, the effects of it were considerably more serious. The rearguards of the 4th Division were still coming in, and exchanging shots with small parties of the enemy as they did so, just before 6 a.m. But there was no awareness that large bodies of Germans were at hand. The lack of divisional cavalry and cyclists was now seriously felt, for the first indication that something was badly amiss was the sight of two French cavalrymen in the distance suddenly turning round and galloping away at top speed to the south-west. Almost immediately afterwards the 1st King's Own of the 12th Brigade were caught by machine-gun fire while drawn up in marching formation. Before they could escape from this, several German batteries also opened fire on them from the north-west. In a few minutes the battalion lost some 400 men. It says volumes for the quality of the infantry of the First Expeditionary Force that they rallied nevertheless, and fought on through the day. The opponents of the 12th Brigade were the 2nd Cavalry Division of von der Marwitz's Cavalry Corps, with their Jägers, machine guns and horse artillery. They pushed the 12th Brigade hard, and began at once to work round its left flank. Soon it became clear that the brigade would have to fall back from its forward position—a matter easier said than done. The King's Own were the first to go, covered by the fire of the 1st Hampshire on the left of the neighbouring 11th Brigade. The Hampshires scored a notable small triumph, when a German battery unlimbered just over 1,000 yards away in the open. With their sights at 1,050 yards, the Hampshires compelled the battery to retire in less than one minute. Other units, however, were in difficulties. The Germans were only 300 yards from the Lanca-shire Fusiliers when they went back, and a platoon of the Innis-killings was wiped out where it stood, with a circle of German dead around it.

After the first surprise, however, the Germans effected little. Their artillery subjected the whole line of the 4th Division to a tremendous bombardment, which grew in volume as the guns of the IV Reserve Corps came up, ahead of their infantry. But there was no moving General Snow's troops. When the Jägers and dismounted cavalry advanced in masses, firing from the hip as they often did, they were cut down and brought to a standstill instantly. A period of deadlock, during which the main activity was by the artillery of both sides, set in along the left flank of Smith-Dorrien's Corps. The first part of his battle had gone extraordinarily well, considering the state in which the II Corps had begun it, and the weight of the forces opposed to it. The danger-point was evidently the right flank, where all hope of any intervention by the I Corps had now been abandoned, and the Germans were free to develop a powerful thrust. Sir John French, one feels, would have done better instead of constantly urging the II Corps to retire, to have tried to procure some diversion from the I Corps. Henry Wilson had told Smith-Dorrien: "Germans fighting Haig cannot fight you." The trouble was that very few Germans were fighting Haig; the retreat of the I Corps on the further bank of the Sambre was relatively undisturbed. It must be noted, however, that the mere act of communicating with Haig presented difficulties enough. Lieutenants Borton and Small of No. 5 Squadron, R.F.C., were sent out to "find" him during the day. Unable to discover a landing-ground in the rear of the I Corps, they "landed between the firing lines in a field protected by a rise in the ground from the direct fire of the enemy. With the aid of a cavalry patrol they succeeded in delivering their message to Sir Douglas Haig, after which they returned to their machine, started up the engine, and flew away in the presence of two Uhlans, who had just ridden into the field." Under conditions such as these, the widening gap between the two British Corps made keeping in touch a nightmare.

It was not long after mid-day that Sir Charles Fergusson saw that the effect of a double enfilade was beginning to make itself felt in his 5th Division. He informed Smith-Dorrien that his men were starting to dribble away, and urged that the retirement should be commenced at once, if it was to be done in an orderly manner. Smith-Dorrien agreed, and his Staff drew up orders for a general withdrawal, which would begin on the right. The first problem was to extract the guns from their advanced positions, many of them actually in the infantry firing line. Some astonishing and splendid deeds were now performed by the 5th Divisional Artillery. The teams of the 11th Battery galloped up during a lull, and got five of their guns away, the sixth team being shot down. Five guns and four howitzers of the 80th and 37th Batteries were also removed, but at the cost of the teams of the 52nd, whose guns had to be abandoned. Shortly afterwards the teams of the 122nd Battery brought the infantry cheering to their feet, as they dashed down the forward slope towards the enemy to bring in their guns. Even the cold pages of the Official History leap to life with this story:

"As they came within view of the enemy, they were struck by a hurricane of shrapnel and of bullets from the machine guns in the Cambrai road; but still they went on. The officer in charge of the teams was killed, one team shot down in a heap before the position was reached, but two guns of the 122nd Battery were carried out without mishap. A third was limbered up, but the horses went down instantly. It was an extraordinary sight: a short wild scene of galloping and falling horses, and then four guns standing derelict, a few limbers lying about, one on the skyline with its pole vertical, and dead men and dead horses everywhere."

It was clear, after this, that there was no point in trying to bring back the guns of the 123rd and 124th Batteries, which were even further forward. They were all abandoned, the breech-blocks being first removed, and the sights smashed. There was, nevertheless, one more brilliant act by the Royal Artillery in this sector; Captain Reynolds of the 37th Battery called for volunteers to fetch in the two abandoned howitzers of the battery. Although the German infantry were no more than 200 yards away, this gallant band limbered up both howitzers. One team was shot down before it could move, but the other escaped. Captain Reynolds and Drivers Luke and Drain all received the V.C. for this act of astonishing bravery.

And now it was the turn of the infantry. The Suffolks—what remained of them—and their supporting detachments of Argyll and Sutherland Highlanders were the first to be overwhelmed. They did not succumb easily. Two officers of the Highlanders were noted, calmly shooting down German after German, and counting out their scores aloud, as if at a rifle competition. The Suffolks had fought for nine hours, making no attempt to withdraw until ordered, and only at last destroyed by attacks from the front, the right flank and the rear. On their left, the Yorkshire Light Infantry of the 13th Brigade did not receive the order to retire. They found themselves isolated, and, like the Suffolks, outflanked. At about half-past three in the afternoon, the remains of this fine battalion were rushed by the enemy. Their stubbornness and their marksmanship played a great part in covering the retirement of the 5th Division. To the rear, down the valley of the Selle, where the German III Corps was now trying to encircle the division, the 1st and 3rd Cavalry Brigades, with their horse artillery, and the Cornwalls and East Surreys who had suffered the first surprise of the day, also performed a valuable covering role. On the left of the division, the retirement of the 15th Brigade was carried out in perfect order. By 6 o'clock in the evening the 5th Division had broken contact with the enemy. Largely because of the devotion of the two battalions which had sacrificed themselves in the forward position, the Germans were held off long enough for there to be no immediate pursuit, and by the end of the day the enemy had had enough. Apart from the 15th Brigade, the 5th Division was in great confusion. On the main road down which it was retiring, the congestion was extremely severe; units were scattered and badly broken up. But there was no irremediable disorder, no panic. General Smith-Dorrien watched the men coming back. "It was a wonderful sight," he says, "—men smoking their pipes, apparently quite unconcerned, and walking steadily down the road—no formation of any sort, and men of all units mixed up together. I likened it at the time to a crowd coming away from a race meeting. . . ."

The retirement of the 3rd Division, in the centre, which at no stage of the day had been so hard pressed as the 5th, was consequently very much easier. Here again, however, the departure of the main body was made much smoother through another act of self-sacrifice by one battalion and a few detachments, arising out of the usual failure to get orders through to troops in the firing line. The artillery also had some losses. The 107th and 108th Batteries each lost an advanced section; that of the 108th fired off its last round as the infantry retired past it, and the officer then disabled the guns. Three teams of the 6th Battery, in the act of withdrawing, were shot down by one lucky German salvo. But it was the 1st Gordon Highlanders, with a party of the 2nd Royal Scots, who did most to foil the German attempt to press the 3rd Division. The order to retreat never reached them in their position to the right of Caudry, in the very centre of the British line. Between 5 and 6 p.m., the crucial period for the withdrawal of the division as a whole, this battalion clung to its position, and repelled attack after attack. Long after the II Corps had left Le Cateau far behind, the Gordons and their Royal Scots comrades were still fighting on their original ground. They marched off finally at midnight, and for a time it looked as though they might make good their escape, but in the darkness they tangled with enemy forces, and after another sharp fight, the remnants of the detachment surrendered at about 3 a.m. on the 27th, in the very midst of the German Army.

The debut of the 4th Division in battle was a memorable one. After their first setback, they fought two divisions of the German Cavalry Corps to a standstill, inflicting on them such casualties that when the IV Reserve Corps arrived in this part of the field it found the cavalry on the defensive, "and several regiments were cowering under cover behind the houses", according to a German report. When the infantry arrived, the cavalry were withdrawn several miles from the battlefield, in the direction of Cambrai, another blunder which ruled out all hope of a vigorous pursuit of the British. The IV Reserve Corps began to show itself in strength at about 4 o'clock in the afternoon, when the 3rd and 5th Divisions were already in the process of retiring. Shortly afterwards Sir Horace Smith-Dorrien had an unpleasant shock. "I suddenly heard very heavy artillery fire away to the north-west, which I reckoned was behind the 4th Division outer flank and feared that the enemy had got behind Snow; but was much relieved, on galloping to a hill about a mile in that direction, to recognise the short sharp crack of the famous 'seventy-fives', and then I knew they were French guns and probably Sordet's, and this they turned out to be." The timely intervention of General Sordet's cavalry was a great help to the 4th Division, which now began the tricky task of extricating itself. In the course of this there were the usual difficulties of bringing away the guns; the 135th Battery removed all its guns by hand; the 27th Battery had to abandon two, but the remaining four dashed through the German shelling during a lull and escaped. The infantry became very dispersed as they withdrew, and once again a number of small parties were left behind. Two companies of the Warwicks had exciting adventures which began that night. They pulled out at about 11 p.m. and, according to Lieutenant B. L. Montgomery, "for three days we marched between the German cavalry screen and their main columns following behind, moving mostly by night and hiding by day. In command of our party was a first class regimental officer, Major A. J. Poole, and it was due entirely to him that we finally got back to the British Expeditionary Force and joined up with our battalion." A party of the King's Own was equally fortunate; two companies of the Dublin Fusiliers, with men from all the divisions that had fought at Le Cateau—and even two soldiers from the 1st

Division, however they may have got there—had a more difficult time. The small remnant of this band finally emerged, many days later, at Boulogne, having marched right across the rear of the German advance. Despite the sufferings and losses of these detachments, there is no doubt that their brave sustained resistance was a major factor in bringing about the safe retreat of the main body of Smith-Dorrien's command. The 4th Division, like the 3rd, was pursued only by shell-fire, and long into the night the retiring British troops were amazed to see German shells still bursting on the positions they had left.

General Smith-Dorrien had every reason to be pleased with the result of his day's work. The Official History sums it up in these words:

> "With both flanks more or less in the air, (II Corps) had turned upon an enemy of at least twice their strength; had struck him hard, and had withdrawn, except on the right front of the 5th Division, practically without interference, with neither flank enveloped, having suffered losses certainly severe, but, considering the circumstances, by no means extravagant. The men looked upon themselves as victors. . . . They had completely foiled the plan of the German commander."

Sir John French, composing his dispatch on September 7th, when the Retreat was over, and the Army was moving forward again, wrote:

> "I cannot close . . . without putting on record my deep appreciation of the valuable services rendered by General Sir Horace Smith-Dorrien. I say without hesitation that the saving of the left wing of the army under my command on the morning of the 26th August could never have been accomplished unless a commander of rare and unusual coolness, intrepidity, and determination had been present to personally conduct the operation."

In his book, however, he tried to disclaim this dispatch: "It was completed, of necessity, very hurriedly, and before there had been time or opportunity to give thorough study to the reports . . . by which alone the full details could be disclosed." The effect of the battle, he then said, was "to render the subsequent conduct of the retreat more difficult and arduous". He gave the losses as "at least 14,000 officers and men, about 80 guns, numbers of machine guns, as well as quantities of ammunition, war material and baggage. . . ."

This reversal of opinion was extraordinary. There is no doubt that French's first impression was that the II Corps had suffered a serious defeat and lasting damage; by the time he wrote the dispatch, he knew that this was not so—the Corps was already playing a leading part in the advance to the Marne; but when he came to write the book, he had set facts aside again. The truth was quite different from what he wrote. "It is undoubtedly a fact," says Smith-Dorrien, "that after Le Cateau we (II Corps) were no more seriously troubled during the ten days' retreat, except by mounted troops and mobile detachments who kept at a respectful distance." As to the casualties, French roughly doubled them; in truth, they amounted to 7,812 officers and men and 38 guns. Von Kluck was convinced that he had been fighting the whole B.E.F.; "six divisions, a cavalry division and several French Territorial divisions opposed the First Army". His miscalculations gave the II Corps twelve hours' start over the First Army, when it began to follow up; this alone justified Smith-Dorrien's wonderful stand.

During the day, G.H.Q. moved again, this time to Noyon; these constant arrivals and departures were a distracting feature, which explains much of the despondency and lack of grip shown by British Headquarters. The I Corps, after its disturbed night, completed its withdrawal successfully, except for a mishap to the 5th Brigade. Its rearguard, the 2nd Connaught Rangers, failed to receive orders to retire, and was ambushed at Le Grand Fayt, with heavy casualties.

The Belgians, who had begun a sortie from Antwerp on the 24th, providing a useful diversion in the rear of the German Armies, now broke it off and retired into the town's defences.

At G.Q.G., Joffre, after much cogitation, decided to organise his new mass of manœuvre on the left as a Sixth Army, and to appoint to it General Maunoury, who had already displayed excellent qualities in Lorraine. In Paris, there was a Ministerial crisis, and M. Messimy was replaced by M. Millerand, whose "tenacity, earnestness and patriotism," says Joffre, "gave me confidence that he would be capable of meeting every emergency that arose".

Behind the German front, the Guard Reserve and XI Corps were beginning their long journey to Russia. They were already too late.

Hindenburg and his Chief of Staff, Ludendorff, had begun the Battle of Tannenberg.

August 26th had been a big day.

8

Lanrezac Fights

ON THE 27th, the aftermath of the Battle of Le Cateau began to make itself felt in all directions. Astonishing misconceptions both of the event and of its results started to circulate, spreading ripples of consternation in wide circles around Smith-Dorrien's three divisions, which alone, at the still centre, remained composed and cheerful. The Staff of II Corps had lost no time in trying to bring order out of the chaos of the first retirement. Standing at cross-roads, they sorted out the mixture of units as it came along: "Transport and mounted troops straight on, 3rd Infantry Division to the right, 5th Infantry Division to the left." The 4th Division, on the extreme left, had a road to itself, down which its main bodies were able to move in reasonably good order, though parts of the division wandered into the zone of the others, and detached parties of all three were to be found all over the place. The feat of Smith-Dorrien's command after their great fight was as wonderful as the battle itself; by dawn on the 28th they had marched 35 miles from Le Cateau to the Somme.

It was as well that von Kluck, now released from the orders of von Bülow, was once again acting on faulty information, and moving his Army away from the B.E.F. The German First Army now began upon the series of futile zigzags across north-western France which ultimately brought it to the edge of disaster; on this day it marched south-west, while the B.E.F. retired due south. This brought the Germans into conflict with the French Territorial divisions of General d'Amade, and to a certain extent compromised Joffre's plan for building up a mass of manœuvre on the left; but it gave the B.E.F. a welcome breathing-space. The troops were by now exhausted to a degree which it is hardly possible to describe in words. Let one story tell the tale for all.

The town of St. Quentin lay directly in the path of the 5th Division; they halted for a couple of hours, and then, with a much-needed meal inside them, went on their way. Stragglers, however, continued to stream into the town, and among them larger parties which had become detached from their proper formations, including at least one half-battalion of the 4th Division, miles off course. Behind the stragglers came a cavalry rearguard, consisting, here, of two squadrons under Major Tom Bridges, with a few French Territorials in support. Bridges' Brigadier had told his officers that they were "in a very tight corner, but must fight it out and die like gentlemen". The Germans, however, were in no thrusting mood; the only glimpse of them was an uncertain one. "During the afternoon a large grey car loaded with ladies came up on to a hill near by and had a good look round. The car was so like a Staff Benz that we thought the sex of the ladies doubtful. We sent a patrol to investigate, but it quickly turned and was gone."

Bridges had arranged with their commander that the French Territorials should dig in, and hold on through the afternoon, but when he returned from his outposts, he found "not a pair of red trousers in sight anywhere. This was my first experience of Allied co-operation. The French, in spite of their gallantry and inherent military qualities, were often unreliable and unpunctual. . . . They came and went like autumn leaves. Where we would hold a position they would abandon it and retake it with a brilliant counter-attack. . . . One had to remember that Marianne was a woman and would keep you guessing. . . ."

Shortly after this the cavalry fell back into St. Quentin, where dreadful scenes met Bridges' eyes: "There were two or three hundred men lying about in the Place and the few officers with them, try as they would, could not get a kick out of them. Worse, Harrison (the interpreter) now reported that the remains of two battalions had piled arms in the railway station and that their Commanding Officers had given a written assurance to the Maire that they would surrender and fight no more, in order to save the town from bombardment. I had to relieve the Maire of this document at once, and sent Harrison back to tell the two Commanding Officers that there was a cavalry rearguard still behind them and they must hurry up and get out. Apparently a meeting was then held, and the men refused to

20 "... the red képi, the long dark-blue capotes and the red trousers of the Second Empire";
French infantry deploying

21 *"... the short sharp crack of the ... 'seventy-five' ..."; a 75 mm. gun in action*

22 *German heavy artillery; a 210 mm. cannon*

23 *". . . the B.E.F. had a quiet day . . .";*
Cavalry resting in bivouac during the retreat

24   ". . . trim, gleaming 18-pounders . . ."; Royal Field Artillery in position

25   ". . . the evident quality of . . . the famous '75s . . ."; French Field Artillery

26   ". . . survivals of . . . the pageantry of the Grand Army . . ."; French Dragoons
with machine gun

27 *". . . their habit of walking as much as they rode . . ."*

28 *". . . still a use for cavalry if properly . . . handled";
British cavalry during the retreat*

BRITISH CAVALRY

29   *Infantry and Cyclists*

30   *Transport, Field Cookers and Highlanders*

31   *Infantry passing through a village*

THE B.E.F. IN RETREAT

32 " . . . kept the gun in action as long as they had a round left to fire." "L" Battery, R.H.A. at Néry, September 1st, 1914

From a print after F. Matania

33   " A German battery barked at us . . ."; British troops under fire at the Marne

march on the ground that they had already surrendered and would only come away if a train was sent to take them. I therefore sent an ultimatum giving them half an hour's grace, during which time some carts would be provided for those who really could not walk, but letting them know that I would leave no British soldier alive in St. Quentin. Upon this they emerged from the station and gave no more trouble."

It had been a difficult moment for Bridges, who was junior to both the Commanding Officers in question. One of them was Colonel Elkington of the Warwicks, the officer who had had all his hair shaved off before coming to France, and who had told Lieutenant Montgomery that he would not need any money on active service. Elkington and the other colonel were cashiered for this episode at St. Quentin. But if truth is stranger than fiction, life is not always so unkind. Elkington joined the French Foreign Legion, and gained a commission in it; he was severely wounded, and won the Legion of Honour. Later, the King reinstated him in the British Army, and awarded him the D.S.O. The whole moral of the affair was that it showed, as Bridges said, "to what extremes good troops will be driven by fatigue".

His own part in the proceedings was not yet concluded: "The men in the square were a different problem and so jaded it was pathetic to see them. If one only had a band, I thought! Why not? There was a toy-shop handy which provided my trumpeter and myself with a tin whistle and a drum and we marched round and round the fountain where the men were lying like the dead, playing the British Grenadiers and Tipperary and beating the drum like mad. They sat up and began to laugh and even cheer. I stopped playing and made them a short exhortation and told them I was going to take them back to their regiments. They began to stand up and fall in, and eventually we moved slowly off into the night to the music of our improvised band, now reinforced with a couple of mouth organs. When well clear of the town I tried to delegate my functions to someone else, but the infantry would not let me go. 'Don't leave us Major,' they cried, 'or by God we'll not get anywhere.' So on we went, and it was early morning before I got back to my squadron."

And so the II Corps came back from Le Cateau, utterly weary, but far from broken in spirit. In the 4th Division, the usual hourly halts were omitted, "for fear that if the whole division were once halted and the men sat or lay down, they would never be got moving again". At 4 a.m. on the 28th the division reached the Somme at Voyennes, where Henry V had crossed the river on his way to Agincourt. The 3rd Division was at Ham, and the 5th at Ollezy; all Smith-Dorrien's infantry were lined up along the Somme. Away on the right, the retreat of the I Corps had increased the gap between the two wings of the B.E.F. from 8 to 18 miles, a serious and disturbing factor. This Corps had been in action during the 27th against the leading units of von Bülow's Second Army, which was trying to envelop the French 5th Army. The 1st (Guards) Brigade, half of which, despite its title, was composed of regiments of the line, had fought a sharp rearguard action at Etreux. There, once again, a sad loss was caused through the usual reason—failure to receive orders to retire. The 2nd Munster Fusiliers, under their ardent commander, Major Charrier, an officer of French descent who had been frantic with joy when the outbreak of war gave him a chance to strike a blow at France's hereditary foe, were cut off. They fought on for twelve hours against at least six German battalions, before the small band of survivors gave in. Charrier himself was killed, with the war that he had greeted only a fortnight old. With his battalion, two guns of the 118th Battery, R.F.A., were also lost. But apart from this incident, the I Corps came away safely, and halted on the high ground south of Guise, on the River Oise.

The tragedy of the day was that the true condition of the tired, hungry, weakened, but far from broken British Army was unknown to anyone except its immediate commanders.

Hair-raising stories began to circulate as early as the evening of the 26th, when at 10.15 Colonel Huguet reported to G.Q.G.: "Battle lost by British Army, which seems to have lost all cohesion. It will demand considerable protection to enable it to reconstitute. . . ." Huguet's temperament was a naturally gloomy one, and despite a long association with the British Army, he seems never to have understood the mental and spiritual processes that animate the British soldier. These rest fundamentally on a stubbornness that frequently, to a Frenchman, resembles dullness, and a sour cheerfulness which, without understanding, can look like its exact opposite.

Take, for example, the story of the officer who met a dozen or so un-shaven, tattered, hobbling British infantrymen, coming back down a road under the command of a sergeant.

"What is your unit?" the officer asked.

The sergeant drew himself up, and replied, with some panache: "We're the Blankshires, sir. First into Mons and last out."

There was a guffaw from behind him. He turned round.

"What's ailing you, Shorty?"

"That's right, sergeant, tell 'em the tale," said Shorty, with a grin.

"Well, what's wrong with that?"

"First into Mons and last out—in at three miles an hour, out at eighteen!"

And a great shout of laughter went up. It takes a very skilled foreign attaché to interpret such a scene correctly. To do him justice, Colonel Huguet, composing his dire tidings, was only reflecting the opinions of G.H.Q. He could be relied upon, however, to give full weight to their most sombre side.

It says volumes for Joffre's personal quality that the day which began for him with the information that his allies, at the most crucial and perilous part of his line, were in a state of collapse, was also the day on which his unfaltering will began to make itself felt among his troops. "A distinct impression gained ground," says Spears, "that the G.Q.G. was laying a firm hand on the direction of affairs, and that drift and vacillation were at an end." At the headquarters of the 5th Army, whose retreat on the 26th had been unmolested, this impression was particularly strong. Joffre was by now taking the measure of Lanrezac. The orders which he sent to the 5th Army early on the 27th were phrased with great care to leave Lanrezac no loophole for evading them:

> "You have expressed to me your intention of throwing back by a counter-offensive, well-supported by artillery, the troops which are following you, as soon as you have left the wooded region where the employment of your artillery is difficult. Not only do I authorise you to carry this out, but I consider such an attack to be indispensable. . . .
>
> "Do not take into account what the English are doing on your left."

The only effect of this order on General Lanrezac was to make him exceedingly angry. All the skills of his devious mind were spent, throughout the day, upon the problem of how not to comply with it. On the telephone to G.Q.G., and in conversation with Joffre's liaison officer, Colonel Alexandre, who twice visited the 5th Army, he resisted strongly. At the end of the day he even went so far as to deliver a violent diatribe to Alexandre, directed against Joffre's whole strategy and G.Q.G. generally. When he learned that Sir John French intended to continue his retreat without pause on the 28th, thereby uncovering the 5th Army's left flank, his temper naturally became very much worse. To Lanrezac, this meant only one thing, that he must also fall back as quickly as possible; to Joffre it meant the exact opposite, that Lanrezac must strike at once to disengage the B.E.F. The difference of opinion between the two men was fast approaching a crisis.

In reply to Huguet's pessimistic message, Joffre had stated his intention to create a diversion with the 5th Army. Later in the day, he had gone himself to Noyon, to see French. Joffre was now embarking upon a remarkable, sustained personal activity which took him constantly up and down the Allied front, rebuking one general, fortifying another, congratulating a third, and giving to all the sense of a Commander-in-Chief firmly in the saddle, cognisant of every local situation. His visit to French, however, produced no immediate effect; it was too early for any useful information to have filtered through to G.H.Q., and too late to change French's mind about the necessity for continuing his retreat. But the meeting was not uncordial, and shortly after it Joffre, on the prompting of Huguet, who was afraid of the effects of these early battles on British opinion, issued a warm message of gratitude to the B.E.F.:

> "The British Army, by engaging itself without hesitation against greatly superior forces, has powerfully contributed towards assuring the security of the left flank of the French Army.
> "It has fought with a devotion, energy and perseverance to which I wish to pay homage, and which I am certain will be manifested in the future in assuring the final victory of our common cause. The French Army will not forget the service rendered. . . ."

It is a wry reflection that neither Joffre nor French, at the time that this message was sent and received, were really aware of the manner in which it had been earned. It was not merely Huguet, who was the bringer of bad news; Colonel Brécard, another of Joffre's liaison officers, after conversations with the British Staff, told him that two of the five divisions of the B.E.F. had been destroyed. He added that, according to Henry Wilson, the British would not be able to fight again for a week, and must have that interval to re-organise. In the evening, Joffre received official confirmation of this state of affairs in a long message from Huguet, embodying the information which had come in to G.H.Q. during the day. It was an astonishing document—and it is no less astonishing that Joffre should have been able to digest it without despair.

> "The situation," said Huguet, "is extremely critical. For the moment the British Army is beaten and is incapable of any serious effort. The right column—1st and 2nd Divisions— . . . still presents some aspects of cohesion; the same may be said of the 4th; but the 3rd and 5th Divisions . . . are now nothing more than disorganised bands, incapable of offering the smallest resistance. . . .
>
> "*Conditions are such that for the moment the British Army no longer exists.** It will not be in a condition to take the field again until it has been thoroughly rested and reconstituted; that is to say, for at least three out of the five divisions, not for some days, or even a few weeks. . . .
>
> ". . . it may even be that the British Government will exact that the whole force *retire to its base at Le Havre** until such time as, having been rested, filled up and re-organised, it will once more be in condition to take the field. But of one thing there can be no doubt whatever . . . the resolution of the British is unshaken, and, indeed they are more determined than ever to recommence fighting as soon as they can.
>
> "It is therefore impossible to count upon this Army for some time. . . ."

It seems inconceivable that any liaison officer should send off a message such as this to his Commander-in-Chief, without making sure that it did, in fact, represent the true situation and the true ideas of the Army to which he was attached. (Spears for example, went to extreme trouble personally to observe the units of the 5th Army, before reporting on them.) It is also inconceivable that any British officer could have allowed this document to pass. Even G.H.Q. could not have said of the I Corps that it still presented "some aspects of cohesion" when, in fact, it had fought no more than a few petty skirmishes. And the suggestion that Britain might

* Author's italics.

pull out of the war—even though it was denied—was a shocking calumny.

Yet, in justice to Colonel Huguet, it has to be said that G.H.Q. was, at this stage, in the agonies of a mental defeat that far surpassed anything suffered by the Army itself. One belief current there, for example, was that the Cavalry Division had been almost totally destroyed at Le Cateau. The truth was that it had suffered exactly 15 casualties in that action. Several days later it was still believed that the 5th Division had lost all, or nearly all its guns. Sir John French personally rebuked Smith-Dorrien, when he reported after the battle, for taking too cheerful a view of the situation; even the sight of some of the II Corps units in retreat, "whistling and singing as they came along", did not relieve French's anxiety. Undoubtedly, the atmosphere in which he had to work himself had got on his nerves; the constant moves of G.H.Q., now at Noyon, made its task the more difficult, and helped to increase the confusion. The Adjutant-General, Sir Nevil Macready, has described the scene at Noyon:

> "A long, dark room—a schoolroom, I think—had been commandeered as the Headquarters office, each of us having a table or two round the walls. Murray, who for the last five days had been severely taxed night and day with a crushing weight of anxiety and practically no sleep, was sitting at a table looking over messages from the front, when he suddenly dropped forward in a dead faint. Our Headquarters medical officer, Cummins, with some staff officers, carried him to a bench and applied restoratives, while Henry Wilson walked slowly up and down the long room, with that comical, whimsical expression on his face, habitual to him, clapping his hands softly together to keep time, as he chanted in a low tone, 'We shall never get there, we shall never get there.' As he passed me I said, 'Where, Henri?' And he chanted on, 'To the sea, to the sea, to the sea.' It was just the way to keep up everybody's spirits, some of the younger members of the staff not always remembering the golden rule of appearing cheerful under any and every turn of circumstances."

No doubt, to Sir Nevil Macready and others at G.H.Q., Wilson's odd behaviour was a tonic; but in other directions he was far from spreading sunshine. On this same day the headquarters of the 4th Division, which had troubles enough, received the following message: "From Henry to Snowball*:—Throw overboard all

* NOTE: Wilson to General Snow.

ammunition and impedimenta not absolutely required, and load up your lame ducks on all transport, horse and mechanical, and hustle along." The same order had been sent to the whole of II Corps, and naturally had a very dismal effect. When Smith-Dorrien heard of it, he countermanded it at once, but was later reproved by French for having done so, and again told that his view of things was too optimistic. The result was that numbers of soldiers were deprived of spare clothes, boots and other small comforts which they were soon to need urgently. Sir William Robertson had fortunately hit upon the sensible idea of making sure of the supply of basic necessities by dumping them along the line of march; it was a wasteful method, but it did mean that the troops were not left entirely unfed and short of ammunition. It also had the unintended effect of causing the enemy to think that the B.E.F. was demoralised. This, to some extent, offset the same conviction among its own leaders.

The sinister element of truth in Huguet's long, improper message to Joffre lay in the reference to the B.E.F. possibly retiring to Le Havre. It was not the British Government that was in any way responsible for this idea—on the contrary, when it was discovered in London it created the utmost alarm—but Sir John French himself. For the rest of the Retreat he clung, with more or less tenacity as the fortunes of war varied, to the incredible notion that he could, in some way, "opt out" of a modern battle—take his Army away to some quiet place, refit it, and return in his own good time. The impact of such thoughts on French soldiers, struggling for the very existence of their nation, may be imagined. If he had never done anything else, the patience and tact with which Joffre opposed, watered down, and finally disposed of this idea were a major contribution to Allied victory.

When August 28th dawned, it was not, however, patience and tact that were the virtues which Joffre first brought into play. What he had been unable to achieve with his Ally by persuasion, he now determined to bring about with his subordinate by compulsion. Colonel Alexandre's experiences on the previous day had made it clear that no amount of telephoning or conveying orders through junior officers would be likely to move Lanrezac; so Joffre decided to call on him in person. He arrived at 5th Army Headquarters about 8.30 a.m., and was immediately struck by the physical appearance of Lanrezac. "Marks of fatigue lined his face; his colour was sallow, his eyes bloodshot. He immediately began, with gesticulations which betrayed his nervous condition, to raise objections to the orders he had received the day before, alleging the tired condition of his troops and the menace which threatened him from the north. . . . I signified to him that in view of all the circumstances it was absolutely necessary for him to make an attack in the direction of St. Quentin. The tone of the conversation became heated. . . ."

Joffre was certainly very incensed with Lanrezac, and made this quite clear to him. When Joffre was in a rage, there were few who could stand up to him. Lanrezac gave way, and said that he was "ready to obey". To make doubly sure, Joffre told his aide, Major Gamelin, to put the order to attack in writing, and signed it immediately: "The 5th Army as soon as possible will attack the troops engaged yesterday against the British. It will cover its right with a minimum of forces and will send out wide reconnaissances in that direction." What this meant, in fact, was one of the most difficult movements that the 5th (or any other) Army could be called on to execute: in the midst of a retreat, it would have, by forced marches, to re-align itself to face almost due west instead of north, and pass immediately to the attack. If it is fair to say that Lanrezac had brought this difficulty on himself by his endless procrastination, it is also fair to remember that it was a real problem, and that he and his staff dealt with it extremely efficiently. Nevertheless, the impression which Joffre brought away with him from his visit to the 5th Army was "painful".

The situation on both flanks of that Army was disturbing. Apart from the continued retreat of the B.E.F., the news from the 6th Army, on the extreme left, where Joffre was hoping to build up his decisive mass of manœuvre, was serious. All contact with two Reserve divisions in the Somme area had been lost, and when finally they were heard of, it was learned that both had had severe fighting and had been driven back. This meant not only that the line of the Somme had been lost but that the whole programme of assembly of Maunoury's Army was in jeopardy. The need for Lanrezac to effect some diversion had become, Joffre saw, greater than ever.

On the right of the 5th Army, too, there were new dangers. A wide gap separated it from its neighbour, the 4th, under General de Langle de Cary. This gap would necessarily grow wider when the 5th Army struck westwards, and Joffre learned with dismay that German forces had been seen heading straight towards it. General de Langle, says Joffre, was a very different man from General Lanrezac: "for at a moment when I was forced repeatedly to stimulate the latter to a more energetic resistance, the former resolutely refused to yield an inch of ground to the enemy". The 4th Army had suffered very severely in its first attack in the Argonne; yet, despite its losses and the shaking that it had received, it had already struck back at the enemy several times, and was in the process of doing so again, with some success. But Joffre was aware that the soldiers must be reaching the limits of their endurance. Much to his regret, he felt forced to order de Langle to break off his action. He also withdrew a part of the 4th Army, which, as the spearhead of the French offensive, had been made very strong, to form a detachment under Foch to cover the gap between it and the 5th. These measures, coupled with an instruction to the 1st and 2nd Armies on his extreme right to "hold out" against the continuing pressure of the Germans in Lorraine, completed Joffre's work on the 28th. There was nothing to show yet for his efforts, but once again on this day he had made his iron will felt all along his line of battle. Only in one quarter was he unable to do anything to avert the manifest peril; he could only hope that the slow fruition of his plans would compel the B.E.F. to rejoin him in the fray.

For the time being, it did not appear that this was very likely. Both the British corps continued their retreat throughout the hot and oppressive day of the 28th. For the II Corps, in particular, the renewed march, with scarcely a pause after their long trek back from Le Cateau, was a grim ordeal. By the end of it, besides fighting two general actions and a number of smaller engagements, they had marched 75 miles since August 23rd. The 3rd Division had marched 68 miles in fifty hours; they were physically worn out, but their spirit was still high. Smith-Dorrien saw most of his troops on the march that day. "They made a brave show," he says. "They could not understand why we were retiring, for they considered they had given as good as they got every time they had met the Germans, and were anxious to go at them again." The II Corps saw nothing of the enemy on this day, and the I Corps very little. The I Corps was moving with both divisions on a single road, which meant double columns; this circumstance, added to the heat and dust, and the inevitable swarms of refugees, made the day an exhausting one for them, and they were glad to come to a halt in the afternoon.

The truth about the Army's condition was far from being appreciated at G.H.Q., but it was beginning to be understood by some people attached to that institution. Brigadier-General Baker-Carr, a distinguished Tank commander later in the war, but at this period serving as a volunteer chauffeur to officers of the Headquarters Staff, was constantly meeting small detached bodies of troops, some of them preserving their organisation, others in straggling parties of ten or a dozen men. It was one of his many jobs, as he pursued his endless travels up and down the line, to help to direct these men back to their proper formations.

" 'Who are you?' I would call out, as a dozen tired and footsore men approached.

" 'We're the sole survivors of the Blankshire Regiment, sir,' an old soldier would reply. 'All the rest got done in yesterday. Not a soul except us is left alive.'

" 'All right. Keep straight on for a couple of miles or more and you will find three or four hundred other sole survivors of your regiment bivouacking in a field.'

"This happened not once, but twenty times. On the first occasion or two, one was inclined to place some credence in the statement of the 'sole survivors', but after a while one became so used to the description that it developed into a joke. It is easy, however, to understand that the expression was employed in the utmost good faith."

There is a ghoulish element in the British character that revels in total disaster, as anyone with experience of the Army, or memories of the stories that used to circulate on the mornings after of the blitz, will agree. No doubt an uncritical acceptance of "sole survivors' " tales helped to build up the false impression of the state of the Army that remained prevalent for some time. Not everyone was in such a good position as Baker-Carr to compare truth with error; and men not present with their units had to be reported as "missing" and reckoned as casualties until they rejoined. It was not difficult to be mistaken; but G.H.Q. was very mistaken indeed.

The only serious threat to the B.E.F. during the day was the possibility of German cavalry thrusting into the now 15 mile-wide gap between the two Corps. This they attempted to do, in two columns, both of which were foiled by the action of the British Cavalry Division, which, so far from being wrecked, was now about to perform some of its best work, covering the retreat of the infantry. The 4th Hussars and "E" Battery, R.H.A., quickly ambushed and checked the western German column; Brigadier General Sir Philip Chetwode's 5th Cavalry Brigade scored a brilliant success against the eastern force. This was composed of the Guard Cavalry Division; near the village of Cérizy they bumped into an outpost line of the Scots Greys who received them with dismounted fire. The Greys were driven in by weight of numbers, but their resistance, supported by "J" Battery, R.H.A., forced the Germans to dismount. Chetwode then deployed the 20th Hussars on the left, and the 12th Lancers on the right, to envelop the Germans, who rapidly began to withdraw. The 12th Lancers soon came upon another body of German horse, advancing in close formation. They compelled this force to dismount by fire action, and stampeded their horses. One squadron of the Lancers was able to work up to within 50 yards of the Germans, and then charged. Seventy or eighty of the enemy were speared, while the Lancers lost only two officers and eight men. The total losses of the 5th Cavalry Brigade did not exceed 30, while those of the enemy may have been ten times as many. They certainly showed little inclination to come to grips with the British cavalry afterwards.

While this was going on, Sir Douglas Haig had learned from the Royal Flying Corps that the Germans were moving in a south-westward direction from St. Quentin, presenting an open flank to his Corps and the 5th French Army as they did so. Haig had by now fully recovered from his nervousness three days before, and urged upon Lanrezac, through a French Liaison officer, the advantages offered by this German manœuvre. He offered the full co-operation of the I Corps, if the French would attack. He did not know, of course, that Lanrezac was already under the firmest orders to do that. Later in the evening the French officer, Captain Helbronner, returned to Haig's headquarters. "I conveyed to him General Lanrezac's thanks and told him of the latter's intentions for the following day. Sir Douglas expressed himself as satisfied, only making reservations concerning the hour at which his infantry was to attack. . . . He asked me to note that he had several heavy batteries at his disposal. He added that it would be necessary that, before participating in the attack, he should obtain Sir John French's sanction to the agreement he had come to with General Lanrezac."

Here, of course, lay the rub. The Staff of the 5th Army had no doubt that they would receive British co-operation, which they were likely to need badly, in view of the complexity of the task that faced them, in their battle the next day. Only Spears, who had more than an inkling of the frame of mind of G.H.Q., doubted. He pointed out the conditional nature of Haig's undertaking, and did his best, without success, to make contact with G.H.Q. Late in the evening his worst fears were confirmed; a message from G.Q.G. announced that Sir John had not agreed to allow Haig to take part in the French attack.

"For the first time," says Spears, "I felt we were in the wrong. . . . The great complaint of the British against General Lanrezac had been that he could not be induced to attack. Now that he was about to do so nothing would persuade the British to co-operate. They were doing as they had been done by. . . . They had been misinformed on every single matter of importance from the numbers of the enemy to the result of the French operations. Where they had looked for support they had found only shadows; schemes, plans, operations, everything had melted away, leaving only one reality— the enemy, who in overwhelming strength and with relentless purpose had driven home blow after blow. . . ."

The percipient words of Kitchener, in his first Instructions, must by now have been tolling like a knell in French's ears—the knell of his high hopes: ". . . the gravest consideration will devolve upon you as to participation in forward movements where large bodies of French troops are not engaged and where your force may be unduly exposed to attack". The whole progress of the war to date could be summed up, from French's point of view, in that sentence. He would take a lot of persuading that the future would be otherwise. Meanwhile his suspicions produced one of the bleakest hours for Allied co-operation of the War.

Few people, either at German Supreme Headquarters, or, indeed, among the still large masses of troops who had not been heavily engaged, now doubted that Germany was well on the way to final victory. The progress of her Army from the frontier had been a continuous advance—less marked, certainly, on the left, but that was largely according to plan; on the right, the First and Second Armies had covered huge distances, always going forward. The frame of mind of these soldiers is revealed in the captured diary of a First Army officer, who wrote on the 28th:

> "This evening we had news of victories gained by von Bülow's Second Army; our souls were filled with joy when the regimental bands played the Hymn of Praise by the light of the moon and of the bivouac fires, and the tune was taken up by thousands of voices. There was general rejoicing and jubilation, and when next morning we resumed our march it was in the hope that we should celebrate the anniversary of Sedan before Paris."

A semi-official report from Supreme Headquarters stated: "The defeat of the English is complete."

On the 28th, new orders reached the German Armies from the Supreme Command, based upon their now firm conviction that the battle in the West had entered its final phase. They opened with these words:

> "His Majesty orders that the German Army advance on Paris."

Von Kluck's First Army was to cover the advance by continuing its course south-west to the lower Seine; the Second Army would march directly on Paris, with the Third covering its left flank; the Fourth and Fifth Armies would swing round Verdun, and invest that fortress; the Sixth and Seventh Armies, in the event of a French withdrawal, would push forward to complete the super-Cannae, the envelopment of both wings of the French line, which von Moltke had never ceased to hope for. The Order was worded in the accents of triumph—and, indeed, the situation, as seen from Coblenz, looked rosy enough. With the next day, however, came the sharp jolt of disappointment; and the unlikely agent of it was General Lanrezac.

The more he thought about their encounter the previous day, the less confidence did Joffre feel in Lanrezac's determination to carry out the plan on which they had agreed. He came to a decision which produced a situation that can have had few precedents or parallels: he decided to return to 5th Army Headquarters, and personally observe Lanrezac's conduct of the battle that was about to begin. If Lanrezac did not seem to be performing his task properly, Joffre was determined to replace him then and there by another man. It was a curious decision; it showed, on the one hand, how strong Joffre's first admiration for Lanrezac must have been, that even with such grave doubts, he was still prepared to give him another chance; on the other hand, it put Lanrezac into a most embarrassing position, having to fight a battle in which he had little faith with, as it were, one eye, and glancing repeatedly over his shoulder with the other, at the silent, watchful, impassive figure of his Chief.

Joffre's first impression of Lanrezac on the 29th was, however, a favourable one: "I had the satisfaction of finding General Lanrezac infinitely calmer than he had been the day before, and above all more master of himself. I was present during the whole morning in his office while he dictated his orders, and I had the impression that he was directing the battle with authority and method." Flanked by his aides, Gamelin and de Galbert, Joffre paced up and down, sometimes in the schoolroom where Lanrezac was working, sometimes along the recreation ground outside, saying nothing, inscrutably observant. To anyone but Lanrezac, it would have been an intolerable position; the strain on the nerves would have been too much. But on him it had an opposite effect: already his strange mind had almost dissociated itself from what he had to do; now the presence of Joffre seemed to absolve him from all responsibility. He became no more than an instrument, and a very effective one. The Battle of Guise was Lanrezac's one great success; paradoxically, it was also the final proof of his entire unfitness for high command.

This was not the only paradox on that day. Joffre's orders to Lanrezac, and Lanrezac's to his Army, were to attack north-westwards, in the direction of St. Quentin, against the flank of von Kluck's

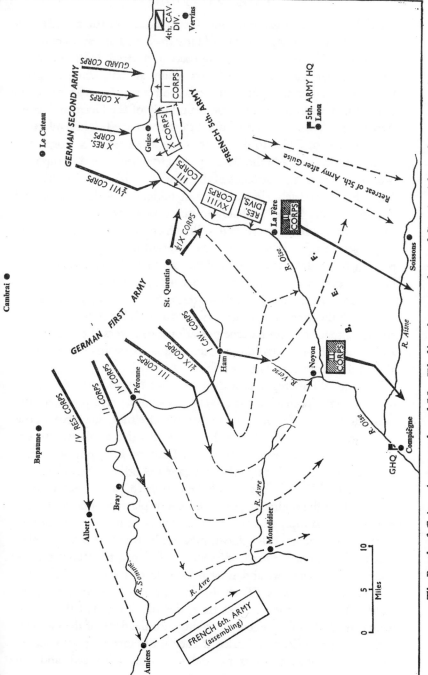

The Battle of Guise, August 29th, and Von Kluck's subsequent change of direction (shown thus – – – →)

First Army, with only covering forces facing north against von Bülow's Second Army, which had hitherto been Lanrezac's constant opponent. Events, however, imposed a different pattern. What happened was this: the French left made, at first, some progress towards St. Quentin, against the relatively small German forces in that area. But as they did so, the main body of the German Second Army came down unobserved upon their contracted right flank from the direction of Guise to the north. Here, the French X Corps was soon in difficulties, and the III Corps had to wheel round in support. Meanwhile German resistance in the west was stiffening. By the time Joffre left Lanrezac's Headquarters at midday, a serious crisis had developed. But Joffre, probably to his surprise, saw Lanrezac meet the occasion with a nerve and skill which anyone might by now have been justified in supposing were absent from his make-up. He pressed his attacks towards St. Quentin to their furthest possible limit; he even went so far as to order his sole reserve, the I Corps, across from his right to push these attacks home. Then, in the nick of time, with the greatest coolness, as the threat to his right developed, and the situation there became precarious, he reversed these orders, and swung the I Corps into a counter-attack towards Guise which altered the entire aspect of the day.

Franchet d'Esperey was a dynamic, but methodical officer. He took his time, preparing the attack of his corps, which was all the more difficult in that it had to advance on either side of the now badly shaken X Corps. When he was satisfied that all was ready, d'Esperey, on horseback, with his Staff around him, put himself at the head of one of his brigades, and gave the order to advance. The long lines of French infantry dashed forward, with their colours flying before the regiments, and their bands playing—one of the last touches of a panoply that was soon to drown in mud and wither on wire entanglements. It is said—it may not be true, but it is typical—that as they went forward, d'Esperey called out to Pétain, once a Staff College lecturer, and now a brigade commander: "*Eh bien, Monsieur le Professeur à l'Ecole de Guerre, que pensez-vous de ce mouvement?*" And now for the first time, the 5th Army had the joy of seeing the backs of the enemy. Striking into the flank of the German Guard Corps, d'Esperey hurled it back a distance of 5 kilometres. Along 25 kilometres of front, the 5th Army advanced, and the

Germans hurriedly withdrew. The battle of St. Quentin had come to nothing; but the Battle of Guise had turned out a striking and deeply significant French success.

For the British Army, August 29th was a day of rest. While the French guns thundered on both sides of them, apart from a few cavalry skirmishes, the British troops saw nothing of the enemy. The II Corps made a short march, which reduced the gap between it and the I Corps to 7 miles; the I Corps enjoyed undisturbed repose. Nobody can grudge the weary British soldiers their well-earned respite; but nobody can take pleasure in the thought of this inactivity, while such momentous events were raging all around. Haig, at least, had assessed the situation correctly, when he had offered to help Lanrezac the day before. But French was immovable.

When he left Lanrezac, in the midst of his battle, pausing only for lunch at a station buffet, Joffre went straight on to visit French, whose headquarters were now at Compiègne. It was not a productive meeting. Joffre urged upon French the vital necessity of the B.E.F. remaining in line with the French formations on either side of it. He spoke again of his plans for an offensive with the 6th Army; he said that Russian action must surely soon relieve the pressure on the Allies in the West. But, he says, "my arguments seemed to produce no effect upon French. Moreover, while I was talking, I distinctly saw his Chief of Staff, Sir Archibald Murray, pulling the skirt of the Field-Marshal's tunic, as if to prevent him from yielding to my insistence." French was set upon further retreat and Joffre could not shift him. "I confess," he says, "that when I departed from Compiègne I was in a very bad humour, for it was certain that the Amiens-Verdun manœuvre was now impossible and another would have to be devised."

Lanrezac had won a victory; but its immediate result was to place his Army in greater peril than before. Drawn forward by its success into an exposed position, totally unsupported on either flank, it was clear that the 5th Army must retire as quickly as possible. But just as Lanrezac had refused to accept responsibility for fighting the battle of Guise, he now washed his hands of its consequences. He was perfectly aware of the danger that he was in, but he refused to withdraw without orders at least as positive as those that had caused him to attack. The following extraordinary dialogue took place on the telephone between Lanrezac and General Belin at G.Q.G., while Joffre was still absent on his travels:

Lanrezac: "Is the 5th Army to delay in the region of Guise-St. Quentin at the risk of being captured?"

Belin: "What do you mean, let your Army be captured, it is absurd!"

Lanrezac: "You do not understand me. I am operating here by the express orders of the Commander-in-Chief to fulfil, so he told me, a mission of public safety. Are the events which have taken place in the last twenty-four hours of such a nature that I am to pursue the operation prescribed to me in spite of the growing risk I am running? I cannot take it upon myself to withdraw on Laon. It is for the Commander-in-Chief to give me the order to retire."

Belin: "I am not entitled to speak for the Commander-in-Chief under these circumstances. I will report to him as soon as he returns."

Lanrezac: "Right. I will remain with a view to resuming if possible my attack on St. Quentin unless the Commander-in-Chief orders me to retire."

One can only suppose that two thoughts were present in Lanrezac's mind when he held this astonishing and well-nigh mutinous conversation: first, the absolute conviction that he would at once receive the necessary order to retire; secondly, a desire to rub Joffre's nose into the fact that, through him, the 5th Army was now in dire peril. The hazards of playing the fool in this manner were soon felt. By an unpredictable accident, an error in the postal service of G.Q.G., the orders which Joffre did, indeed, send off as soon as he became aware of what was happening, were not transmitted to Lanrezac. Not until 7 a.m. the next day, when a telephonic confirmation came through, did the 5th Army begin its retreat again. Fortunately, the blow that it had struck at Guise saved it from immediate pressure by the German Second Army; but it was a near thing.

On the right of the 5th Army, General de Langle's troops were now falling back with their customary steadiness; and Foch was in the process of organising his detachment to cover the wide gap between de Langle and Lanrezac. But the main news of the day, disturbing in some ways, yet gratifying in others, was that von

Kluck's attacks on Maunoury's 6th Army, away to the left round Péronne, which had been severe and ominous all the morning, had died away at noon. Shortly afterwards German columns were seen, apparently marching northwards from this area. It was quite clear, and good news, that Lanrezac's victory had caused this about turn by the German First Army. That Army now swung through 90 degrees from the south-westward course which it had been following, to a south-eastward direction calculated to place it on Lanrezac's flank. Von Kluck's fatal decision to set aside the instructions of the Supreme Command were based on his conviction that the B.E.F. was finished, and his failure to comprehend the significance of Maunoury's role. His movement, though gravely threatening the 5th Army, gave to the 6th the breathing space for assembly which it urgently needed, and which ultimately brought about his downfall. But for the time being the return of the First Army to the vicinity of the B.E.F. confirmed Sir John French's fears, and made him more than ever determined to take his Army out of the line of battle. The next five days would contain, for Joffre, the final crisis of the campaign. It was a matter of timing. The key question was: would the opportunity for Maunoury to strike his blow occur before French's misgivings robbed it of the chance of success?

9

The Climax

AUGUST 30th was another day of intense heat, in that remarkable summer of 1914. Spears was on the road early, visiting G.H.Q. at Compiègne, to make yet another attempt to persuade French to slow down his retreat. Despite the heat, says Spears, French "was certainly one of the coolest and calmest people at G.H.Q." But this calm was misleading—it was that of a man whose worst fears have been realised, and who has made up his mind to act accordingly. In the local sense, Spears did not entirely fail in his mission, for a brief halt was called in the retirement of the B.E.F. But only a few hours later, when French had learned that both the 5th and 6th Armies were continuing to withdraw, he telegraphed to Joffre:

> "I feel it very necessary to impress upon you that the British Army cannot under any circumstances take up a position in the front line for at least ten days. . . . You will thus understand that I cannot meet your wishes to fill the gap between the 5th and 6th Armies. . . ."

And a little later Huguet telegraphed again:

> "Field-Marshal wishes to withdraw his troops behind the Seine, zone Mantes, Poissy, St. Germain, to refit. Wishes to know whether this proposal has the consent of the military authorities and of the Government; in event of affirmative British officers will be sent to prepare billets. . . . The Field-Marshal proposes that Le Mans be chosen as advanced base in place of Amiens."

A glance at a map will show what this portended: the zone selected for the B.E.F. during its ten-day rest lies south of the Seine, *west* of Paris; Le Mans is in the French province of Maine, to the south-west; the rear base finally chosen for the Army was St. Nazaire, in Brittany. For a time there was even talk of La Rochelle. It was as well that Sir William Robertson had laid his plans for a

change of bases so well in advance; even so, the speed and efficiency with which the switch was made deserves all praise. But the high standard set by the Q.M.G.'s department does not alter the fact that G.H.Q. as a whole was now in the grip of a despondency and unrealism which, left to run their course, would have spelt ruin for the Allies.

His decision once taken, French's orders began to flow out from G.H.Q. They produced immediate repercussions in London, and Kitchener telegraphed to French to know what was the meaning of them. The reply that he received was illuminating:

> "I cannot say that I am happy in the outlook as to the further progress of the campaign in France. My confidence in the ability of the leaders of the French Army to carry this campaign to a successful conclusion is fast waning, and this is my real reason for the decision I have taken to move the British forces so far back. . . ."

French could see no other reason for his Allies' failure than "defective higher leading". It is one of the ironies that he should reach this conclusion just when that very leadership was showing every sign of becoming effective. To Joffre, of course, his attitude was calamitous: "It was quite evident that the offensive battle I had conceived on the 25th was now out of the question in the form I had planned." With our post-1940 knowledge of what can be the outcome of such a sequence of defeats and disappointments, it is impossible to withhold from Joffre every admiration for the fortitude with which he faced his sea of troubles. Not for a moment did he consider giving way. His mind began to work at once on new expedients—"re-editing the manœuvre which we had essayed originally in a north-easterly direction by debouching from the Meuse". In other words, with his out-flanking manœuvre on the extreme left apparently still-born, he reverted for a time to the idea supported by Berthelot, of striking a blow from the left-centre which would cut off the enemy's right wing from the rest of his forces. It would be a desperate chance, but it is the mark of an invincible mind to snatch at all chances, rather than accept defeat.

For the whole of Joffre's centre and left, the 30th was a day of retreat. General Maunoury was glad of the opportunity to pull his exhausted

Reservists and Territorials away from the enemy, giving them time to rest a little and reorganise. The B.E.F. narrowed the gap between the I and II Corps to 6 miles, which was also satisfactory; it had no contact with the enemy at all. On this day a British III Corps was formed, under General Pulteney, comprising the 4th Division and the 19th Infantry Brigade. The 5th Army, starting late, had a difficult time as it withdrew, particularly on its left flank. The Army escaped, but it was a trying time for all concerned. On its right, Foch's detachment fell back across the Aisne, tired, but in good order; while to the right again, de Langle was protesting that it would injure the morale of his troops if they had to go on retreating, since they asked nothing better than to be allowed to attack again.

It was on this day that Joffre informed the Government that Paris was likely to be seriously menaced, and recommended that the Government itself should move to Bordeaux. This step was necessary, if the Army's liberty of manœuvre was to be preserved; but it had a bad moral effect on the population of the capital, and did more to depress the French people than any other news that had yet reached them. Joffre himself had reason for depression, in the realisation, from intercepted German wireless messages, that his Russian Allies, on whom he had counted greatly, had suffered a terrible catastrophe at Tannenberg, where the whole of their Second Army had been destroyed. Its commander commited suicide the next day. But Joffre was able to comfort himself with the reflection that, nevertheless, "the Russians had rendered us exactly the service I had expected of them; for, as I learned the next morning, at the very moment that this bad news arrived from Tannenberg, two German army corps were leaving our front on their way to East Prussia".

This was not the only example of the Supreme Command's ineptitude, for it was on this day that, accepting a report from von Bülow that the French were decisively beaten, von Moltke concurred in von Kluck's manœuvre to the south-east. One week had passed since the Battle of Mons; before the end of another this fateful act would have opened the way to the Battle of the Marne.

Once again, on the 31st, the B.E.F. had a quiet day, with only a few minor cavalry skirmishes to indicate the presence of the enemy. By contrast, there was tremendous telegraphic activity between G.H.Q.

and London. It began with a long telegram from Sir John French to Lord Kitchener, a message so astonishing and contradictory in its content that the Government must have been impelled to wonder whether the Commander-in-Chief was not suffering from some mental collapse. After a summary of the general situation, referring to the withdrawal of the French Armies on his flanks, French continued:

> "I have let [Joffre] know plainly that in the present condition of my troops I shall be absolutely unable to remain in the front line. . . . I have decided to begin my retirement tomorrow in the morning behind the Seine, in a southwesterly direction west of Paris. *This means marching for some 8 days without fatiguing the troops at a considerable distance from the enemy.* . . ."*

Then French proceeded to criticise Joffre's plan, adding: "I should like to have assumed a vigorous offensive at once, and this has been represented to him. . . ." And he concluded: "I have no idea of making any prolonged and definite retreat."

What was anyone to make of this? The Army, it appeared, was too weak to remain in the front line; yet French wanted a vigorous offensive. He was proposing to retreat for eight days "at a considerable distance from the enemy", but this was not to be regarded as "prolonged" or "definite". Kitchener, obviously alarmed, replied at once:

> "I am surprised at your decision to retire behind the Seine. Please let me know if you can all your reasons for this move.
> "What will be the effect of this course upon your relations with the French Army and on the general military situation? Will your retirement leave a gap in the French line or cause them discouragement, of which the Germans might take advantage to carry out their first programme of first crushing the French and then being free to attack Russia. . . ?"

Kitchener then showed the Cabinet French's message. Their reaction caused him to follow up his telegram with a second:

> "The Government are exceedingly anxious lest your force, at this stage of the campaign in particular, should, owing to your proposed retirement *so far from the line,** not be able to co-operate closely with our Allies and render them continuous support.

* Author's italics.

They expect that you will, as far as possible, conform to the plans
of General Joffre for the conduct of the campaign. . . ."

He concluded by saying that the Government had "all possible
confidence in your troops and yourself", which was polite, but
passes belief.

These two telegrams drew from French an answer which could do
nothing but increase the Government's anxiety. "If the French go on
with their present tactics," he said, "which are practically to fall back
right and left of me, usually without notice, and to abandon all idea
of offensive operations, of course, then, the gap in the French line
will remain and the consequences must be borne by them. . . ." The
B.E.F., he went on to say, was hardly in a condition to withstand the
attack of even one German Corps. An offensive movement was,
however, open to the French, "which would probably close the gap
by uniting their inward flanks. But as they will not take such an
opportunity I do not see why I should be called upon again to run
the risk of absolute disaster in order a second time to save them."
The II Corps, he went on, was "shattered"; and the French retirements made it impossible for him to reorganise. He admitted that his
supply and lines of communication were "excellent in every way";
finally, he agreed to halt around Nanteuil "if the French armies are
not driven south of their present situation".

Altogether, a less satisfactory document could hardly have been
penned. The note of pique bordering on childishness was probably
the most disturbing feature of it for the Government, with its grave
suggestion of mental unbalance. Strategically, the idea that the
French might "close the gap by uniting their inward flanks" is a
revelation of how far French was from understanding the big scheme
which Joffre had been attempting to bring off. There is nothing
about this correspondence in French's book; there, he tries to make
out that the disagreement was only over his refusal to "stand and
fight", and that he was entirely justified in resisting what he calls
"undue interference by the Government at home with the Commander of an Army in the field". But his whole account, apart from
the omissions and distortions by which he sought to justify himself,
is clouded by his resentment at what followed. For the last passage in
this exchange of telegrams came from Kitchener, in the early hours
of September 1st:

"I am coming to see you this morning to talk over the situation, as I find it very difficult to judge. Please send a telegram to the Embassy at Paris immediately, stating where we can most conveniently meet."

All through the Armies, whether dressed in khaki or in blue, from the footsore, hungry, dirty soldiers to the highest Staffs, depression was beginning to take hold, as the Retreat continued and showed no sign of coming to an end. At G.Q.G. Joffre noted that "only a few of my officers had maintained their calm intact". The Reserve divisions of the 5th Army had become little better than a mob; even in the Active formations, the great loss of officers and N.C.O.s was having its effect. There was a bad scare in the 5th Army on the 31st, when it was learned that a German cavalry Corps was cutting in right across the Army's line of retreat. A little more energy on the part of this German Corps—von Richthofen's—might have produced a total and irremediable disaster, for its objective was the Aisne bridges over which the 5th Army would have to retire, and from which it was still separated by many miles. Only by the narrowest margin was the crisis averted—and partly because the Germans, too, were in trouble. A wireless message from their Guard Cavalry Division was intercepted, saying that their horseshoes were practically worn out, and asking for nails to be rushed to them.

This incursion of German cavalry produced much confusion, and greatly added to the worries and misconceptions of the Staffs. Colonel Seely, recently Secretary of State for War, and now serving on French's Staff, has left an impression of these strange and disturbing times. He was returning from the 5th Army front to Compiègne, unaware that these German horsemen had worked in between the French and Haig's I Corps. "There happened to be a thick fog as I drove along at about 10 o'clock at night. In front of me I saw cavalry on the move. I was glad to see them, thinking they were our own, but when I got about half-way along the little column I heard the men conversing in German! They were lolling in their saddles utterly exhausted; some of them were actually asleep on their holsters. As I neared the head of the troop someone shouted: 'Wer da?' With my heart in my mouth, I replied, very loudly and determinedly: 'Grosse general stab', and proceeded on my way."

Quite apart from such encounters, the nights were eerie enough.

There were constant reports and rumours of enemy incursions, and spies signalling. The very sky itself took on a lurid and menacing hue. Major Small, of the ever-active Royal Flying Corps, wrote: "On returning from late reconnaissances in the dusk, it was most interesting to watch the local fighting in the roads between their vanguards and our rearguards. The spreading of fires all over the country around Compiègne Forest was a more curious sight than even the later trench offensive, the fires spreading like long flaming worms along the main road, as the Huns fired each village they went through. The northern portion of Compiègne Forest was blazing at this date."

Sir John French never forgave Lord Kitchener for what happened at their meeting on September 1st. They met in Paris, and Sir John immediately had a rude shock: "Lord Kitchener arrived on this occasion in the uniform of a Field-Marshal, and from the outset of his conversation assumed the air of a Commander-in-Chief, and announced his intention of taking the field and inspecting the troops." Sir John had not sought for this meeting, and did not desire it: "I deeply resented being called away from my headquarters at so critical a time. Two important actions were fought . . . during this day, over which there was no one to exercise any co-ordinating control." The sight of Kitchener, a senior Field-Marshal, in uniform, was the last straw. The first part of their interview, in the presence of the British Ambassador in Paris, did not go well, and Kitchener quickly broke it off to speak to French privately.

Since, of the two men who now conducted this vital *tête-à-tête*, one died without leaving an account of it, and the other became so inflamed that his report cannot be relied upon, it is not possible to say exactly what happened behind those closed doors in Paris. French says: "When we were alone [Kitchener] commenced by entering a strong objection to the tone I assumed. Upon this I told him all that was in my mind. I said that the command of the British forces in France had been entrusted to me by His Majesty's Government; that I alone was responsible to them for whatever happened, and that on French soil my authority as regards the British Army must be supreme until I was legally superseded. . . . I further remarked that Lord Kitchener's presence in France in the character of a soldier could have no other effect than to weaken and prejudice my position in the eyes of the French and my own countrymen alike. I reminded him of our service in the field together some thirteen years before, and told him that I valued highly his advice and assistance, which I would gladly accept as such, but that I would not tolerate any interference with my executive command and authority so long as His Majesty's Government chose to retain me in my present position. I think he began to realise my difficulties, and we finally came to an amicable understanding."

This last statement was certainly untrue. Six days later French was writing to Winston Churchill: "I can't understand what brought Kitchener to Paris. . . . His visit was really most unfortunate. . . ." Four days after that, following a soothing reply from Churchill, he was prepared to admit: "I fear I was a little unreasonable about K. and his visit, but we have been through a hard time, and perhaps my temper isn't made any better by it!" But by 1919, when he wrote his book, French had reverted again to his first resentment: "It is very difficult for any but soldiers to understand the real bearing and significance of this Paris incident. If the confidence of the troops in their commander is shaken in the least degree, or if his influence, power and authority are prejudiced by any display of distrust in his ability to conduct operations, however slight the indications of such distrust may be, the effect reacts instantly throughout the whole Army. . . . Then again there was the effect which might have been produced on the French. . . . Fortunately . . . Lord Kitchener realised his mistake and left Paris that night." "Lord Kitchener," French concludes, "came to Paris with no other object than to insist upon my arresting the retreat, although no sign of a halt appeared at any part of the Allied line. . . . It was difficult to resist such pressure. Fortunately I was able to do so."

This was not so. We have, as it happens, two pieces of documentary evidence which destroy this image of the gallant soldier standing up for vital principles against unwarrantable interference. We know that it was not French's retreat as such that took Kitchener to Paris, but the manner in which he proposed to conduct it. As Churchill put it to him on September 4th: "The Cabinet was bewildered by your telegram proposing to *retire from the line**. . . .

* Author's italics.

We feared that you and Joffre might have quarrelled, or that something had happened to the Army of which we had not been informed . . ." And this is borne out by the telegram which Kitchener sent to the Government after the meeting, and of which he sent a copy to French: "French's troops are now engaged in the fighting line, *where he will remain** conforming to the movements of the French Army, though at the same time acting with caution to avoid being in any way unsupported on his flanks." Kitchener added to French: "I feel sure you will agree that the above represents the conclusions we came to; but in any case, until I can communicate with you further in answer to anything you may wish to tell me, *please consider it as an instruction**. . . ." Clearly, it was French who was overruled. Indeed, he wrote to Joffre that day himself, through the French Minister of War, proposing a defensive battle along the Marne, and offering to hold his ground on that line "for as long a time as the situation requires", provided only that his flanks were not left exposed.

It was the uniform that upset him. Touchy at any time, he found the presence of the senior Field-Marshal intolerable. The reasons that he puts forward do not bear a moment's scrutiny. The notion that the sight of England's premier serving soldier, the rock-like figure on whom the whole nation based its will to win, the man whose picture on posters throughout the land brought in a million recruits to the Army, could do anything to injure the morale of the B.E.F., is ludicrous. Nor could it have injured French; only strengthened him, if he and Kitchener had seemed to be in accord. French does himself an injustice. His own rapport with the troops was never questioned. It was the best thing about him, that, among the soldiers, his tough, rubicund figure, his terse, military speech, and the warm emotion that always ran through him like electricity at contact with his men, made him respected and loved far beyond what the historian must consider his true deserts to be. In a war famous for remote, aloof generals, this quality of French's is worth remembering.

But there were more cogent reasons for not wishing Kitchener to inspect the Army—reasons unconnected with military protocol. If Kitchener had gone round, he would inevitably have met the two Corps commanders, and what would they have said to him? What

* Author's italics.

would Smith-Dorrien, the man whom Kitchener had appointed against French's wishes, and whom French had already admonished for being too cheerful, have said, when Kitchener asked him, as he would be bound to do, about the "shattered" state of the II Corps? He could only have replied that the corps was tired, certainly, and in need of reinforcement, but far from shattered. What would Haig have said? Would he have referred to the events of three days previously, when he had offered his help to Lanrezac, and French had refused to permit him to make good his promise? He could hardly have failed to say something about that lost opportunity. And above all, the troops themselves, to a practised eye like Kitchener's, who had seen what they could do after long, brutal marches under the African sun and in India, would have been tremendously exhilarated at the sight of his massive frame among them, and would entirely have spoilt G.H.Q.'s case. It is impossible to resist the conclusion that Sir John was being, at the very least, disingenuous.

Nor can one make much of his "resentment" at being away from his Army on a day when it was actively engaged, and needed "co-ordinating control". The two large actions of the B.E.F. in the campaign so far had both been fought with a conspicuous absence of co-ordinating control by French or any other part of G.H.Q. Perhaps Kitchener would have learned this too. In any case, the Army was managing very well.

There could hardly be a greater discrepancy than that between the account of the B.E.F.'s condition which French gave to the Government, and the actual performance of those parts of it which clashed with the enemy on September 1st. On that day, von Kluck, once more aware that the British were near him, but still believing, in the words of a semi-official German report that: "The English Army is retiring on Paris in the most complete disorder", decided to finish with the B.E.F. once and for all, and accordingly swung his columns south. Leading them was the Cavalry Corps of von der Marwitz, whose 4th Cavalry Division arrived at 5.30 a.m. at the village of Néry, and beheld a sight that every soldier hungers for. From the heights on the western side of the village they were able to look down and see, in the misty valley below, the 1st Cavalry Brigade and

"L" Battery, R.H.A., watering their horses and having breakfast. A patrol of the 11th Hussars dashed in with the news that German cavalry were about, and almost instantly a storm of fire from rifles, machine guns and the twelve artillery pieces of the German division burst over the 1st Cavalry Brigade at a range of little more than 600 yards. It was a complete surprise.

The horses of the Queen's Bays stampeded at once. "L" Battery was limbered up and standing in mass, presenting a wonderful target. Men and horses began to go down fast; the battery commander was hit. Captain Bradbury, the second-in-command, managed to get three guns unlimbered and turned round to answer the German fire. One of them was put out of action instantly by a direct hit, and almost immediately afterwards a second was silenced, the whole detachment being wiped out. The last available gun of "L" Battery then began its contest with the twelve German guns on the heights. Gunner after gunner went down, until only Captain Bradbury, Sergeant Nelson and Battery-Sergeant-Major Dorrell were left to work the gun. Captain Bradbury was mortally wounded, fetching ammunition, but the other two kept the gun in action as long as they had a round left to fire. All three won the Victoria Cross.

Meanwhile, the cavalry of Brigadier-General Briggs' brigade were reacting sharply; two squadrons of the 5th Dragoon Guards made a dismounted attack on the enemy's right flank, and, as the sun began to burst through the mist, the 4th Cavalry Brigade, with "I" Battery, R.H.A., appeared on the scene, followed by various infantry units. "I" Battery engaged the enemy with immediate effect, and eight of the twelve German guns were abandoned where they stood, to be captured shortly afterwards by the 1st Middlesex. The 11th Hussars pursued the retiring enemy, and took 78 prisoners, from whom it was possible to identify every unit of the German 4th Cavalry Division. The tables had been completely turned on the enemy; what should have been the severe defeat of a British brigade ended with the smashing of a German division. British casualties at Néry amounted to 135 officers and men, of whom 5 officers and 49 men belonged to "L" Battery.

Further to the east, the infantry of the 2nd Division, retiring through the thick forest of Villers Cottérêts, had greater difficulties.

The rearguard of the division was the 4th (Guards) Brigade. From 10.45 a.m. until 2 p.m. this brigade was engaged in hard, confused fighting in the woodlands. For the 1st Irish Guards, it was an historic moment, for this was the first serious action of the regiment; but it was also tragic, for their Commanding Officer, Colonel Morris, was killed. It was tragic also for the 2nd Grenadiers, who had two platoons surrounded and killed, fighting to the last man. The 4th Brigade lost over 300 officers and men, and the 6th Brigade, which covered its retirement, lost another 160. Public imagination is a strange thing: Villers Cottérêts is practically forgotten, except by regimental historians, while Landrecies has become a legend, and yet the latter was, by comparison, a trifling affair.

At the end of the day, the gap which had existed between the two wings of the B.E.F. since the 25th was closed at last. It had shaken off von Kluck's attempt to catch it—his Army only averaged a 10-mile advance a day. Reports from the Royal Flying Corps continued to show that the main body of the German First Army was marching south and south-east, away from that left flank which had been such an endless source of anxiety. There were, however, new anxieties in plenty. The whole area in front of the B.E.F., and on its right, was thick with German cavalry, small parties of whom filtered constantly through the lines, causing alarm and confusion. At Dammartin, where G.H.Q. had just settled, there were amazing scenes, dryly recorded by Baker-Carr: "The departure from Dammartin was a panic-stricken flight. Rumours of thousands of Uhlans in the woods nearby arrived every moment. Typewriters and office equipment were flung into waiting lorries, which were drawn up in serried ranks in front of the château. It was a pitch-black night, lit up by a hundred dazzling headlights. With much difficulty I collected my quota of passengers, and got clear of the seething mass of vehicles. having deposited my load at the next halting-place, I returned once more to Dammartin, where I had left some washing which I could ill afford to lose. Everything in the little town seemed quiet and peaceful, so, seeking out my previous billet, I went to bed and enjoyed a good night's sleep." Sir Henry Wilson was noted, being his usual sardonic, imperturbable self. Sir William Robertson was just sitting down to a roast leg of mutton when the alarm came; it had to be wrapped in newspaper and taken away on the floor of a lorry. Phlegmatic as ever, Robertson commented: "It was none the worse next day, except for being cold."

But the worst case was that of Sir Nevil Macready, the Adjutant-General. Colonel Cummins, the medical officer, tells how, having been loftily told by an omniscient-looking Staff Officer that: "There are *no* Germans within twenty miles of Dammartin", he went back to his work. "A few hours later, towards 7.30 p.m. . . . I went up to Sir John French's quarters as there was one of his orderlies ill and I had intended to see how he was getting on. To my surprise, however, I found the building deserted and learnt from some orderlies that the General Staff had left Dammartin. This struck me as queer, as I had only just left Colonel O'Donnell on his way to dine with the Adjutant-General. I hurried down to Sir Nevil Macready's quarters and found him sitting down to dinner with his staff, and quite innocent of any idea that G.H.Q. was on the move! On hearing that the General Staff had departed he showed more annoyance than surprise. . . ." No, perhaps the day on which G.H.Q. abandoned the Adjutant-General would not have been the best for taking Lord Kitchener round.

To the left of the British Army, General Maunoury's troops were also in conflict with von Kluck's columns as they swung south. The 5th Army completed its crossing of the Aisne, with scenes of dreadful disorder in some places. The voice of General Lanrezac was heard, at one time, upraised for all to hear, proclaiming: "*Nous sommes foutus! Nous sommes foutus!*" The 5th Army was beginning to acquire a hunted feeling. A gap of 25 miles existed between it and the B.E.F., and this Joffre now set about filling by the creation of a new French cavalry Corps under General Conneau.

It was on September 1st that he issued his *Instruction Générale No. 4*, the first presage of the counterstroke that he now felt to be imminent. He also placed Maunoury under General Galliéni, the commander of the Paris garrison. This relieved Galliéni's proper apprehensions about the safety of the capital, and opened the way for the later use of the Paris garrison in the offensive which Joffre was planning. The Instruction itself, however, shows that his mind was still fixed upon the alternative manœuvre to which it had turned after his unsuccessful meeting with French on the 29th—the attack by the

3rd, 4th and 5th Armies against the inner flank of the German right wing. Information that came in during this day, partly from the Royal Flying Corps and partly from a map found on a wounded and captured German officer, proved to be of exceptional importance. It showed that von Kluck was marching away from Paris, and beginning to expose an open flank to the Allied forces in the neighbourhood of the city. Instruction No. 4 had hardly gone out before Joffre found himself wondering again whether it might not be possible, after all, to carry out the blow he had always favoured against the extreme flank of the enemy. All would depend upon the British.

The B.E.F. made shorter marches during the retirement on the 2nd, but they were exhausting because of the suffocating heat and the constricted country through which the Army was now moving. There were reports of enemy cavalry ahead of and between the columns, but the only evidence of these was of a kind that proved beyond doubt how severely damaged the German 4th Cavalry Division had been at Néry. The four guns which the enemy had succeeded in withdrawing from that action were found abandoned in a wood, and though the British were frequently told that there were German horsemen nearby, these always vanished in haste when any attempt was made to find them. A picture of the B.E.F. at this stage of the Retreat has been left by one of the French civilians who saw it pass: "The soldiers, phlegmatic and stolid, march without appearing to hurry themselves; their calm is in striking contrast to the confusion of the refugees . . . as sportsmen who have just returned from a successful raid, our brave English eat with a good appetite, drink solidly, and pay royally those who present their bills . . . and depart at daybreak, silently like ghosts, on the whistle of the officer in charge." General Smith-Dorrien noted in his diary: "The troops have quite recovered their spirits, and are getting fitter every day, and all they want is the order to go forward and attack the enemy."

The Germans were feeling the strain; on this day one of von Kluck's officers wrote: "Our men are done up. For four days they have been marching 24 miles a day. . . . The men stagger forward, their faces coated with dust, their uniform in rags, they look like living scare-crows. They march with their eyes closed, singing in chorus so that they shall not fall asleep on the march. The certainty of early victory and of triumphal entry into Paris keeps them going and acts as a spur to their enthusiasm. Without this certainty of victory they would fall exhausted. They would go to sleep where they fell so as to get to sleep somehow or anyhow. It is the delirium of victory which sustains our men, and in order that their bodies may be as intoxicated as their souls, they drink to excess, but this drunkenness helps to keep them going. Today after an inspection the general was furious. He wanted to stop this general drunkenness. We managed to dissuade him from giving severe orders. If there were too much severity the army would not march. Abnormal stimulants are necessary to make abnormal fatigue endurable. We will put all that right in Paris." The British and French troops, making equally long marches in retreat, had no prospect of victory to stimulate them, and, for the most part, managed to keep going without the aid of excessive drink. Undoubtedly, it was the influence of alcohol that caused the Germans to commit many of their acts of vandalism and brutality of which there is more than sufficient evidence.

For Joffre, each day now posed the question: "Has the time come?" His Armies, after all, were largely intact: "The great battle which was to decide the fate of the war had not yet been fought; there had taken place, so far, only partial engagements; these, in some cases had turned out to our advantage, in others to our disadvantage. But by continuing this retreat indefinitely, we would end by giving the appearance of a beaten army before even any decisive action had been fought. In addition to all this, the retirement was delivering a large portion of our territory into the hands of the enemy, and it was my duty to reduce this painful sacrifice to its narrowest limits." There was much discussion at G.Q.G. What finally decided the matter was the condition of the troops. None of them were yet in a condition to pass straight to a major counter-offensive. Moreover, time was still needed to complete the transfer of units from the right flank to the left. "Did all this present a combination of circumstances favourable for fighting a decisive battle? Certainly not." The retreat must go on, but the counter-stroke would not be long delayed.

One thing was certain, Sir John French's scheme for a stand on the Marne would not do. Through the Minister of War, and to French personally, Joffre wrote, explaining that, owing to the position of the 5th Army, he could not accept battle, and asking the B.E.F. to co-operate in the defence of Paris. The tone of his reply to French was friendly, conciliatory and respectful. He promised to keep the British Commander-in-Chief fully informed. French responded with the generosity of which he was capable in his best moments; replying the next day, he said: "You can count on my most cordial co-operation on all points." Much credit is due to Joffre for the tact with which he handled French at this juncture, but as Spears remarks, "the fact remains . . . that this better understanding was due to the insistence of both Governments. Necessity had compelled them to assert themselves and the results were excellent."

In another direction, too, Joffre had to exert tact and discretion. The French Government had left Paris; German cavalry patrols were prowling around the outskirts of the capital; barricades were being thrown up; Galliéni was becoming more anxious than ever. Maunoury's Army had again been in conflict with the enemy around Senlis, and the B.E.F. did not seem to promise strong support. "If Maunoury cannot hold out," Galliéni told Joffre, "we are in no condition to resist." And he asked that the field armies should defend the northern and eastern fronts of Paris. This put Joffre in a quandary; he had no intention of being involved in a static defence of the capital; but at the same time, he did not want to reveal his real plans to anyone at this stage. Some hint of them was contained in an explanatory note which he issued on Instruction No. 4, in which he spoke of Maunoury operating towards Meaux, in the forthcoming offensive. He urged on Galliéni the need to pull back the 6th Army as quickly as possible into its defence positions in the meantime, and with this Galliéni had to be satisfied.

Von Kluck had wasted half a day trying to catch the British, and only when he realised that this was impossible did he turn again to the south-east. His erratic movements were a great source of perplexity to the Allied Intelligence officers, but they fathomed their enemy's plans far better than von Kluck's staff were able to do. He, for example, completely failed to identify Maunoury's troops at Senlis as the Army which he had been fighting on the 29th. The German Supreme Command now issued new orders to the First and Second Armies, to drive the French south-eastward, away from

Paris, and von Kluck began to conform accordingly. Both Armies were now entering the depths of the net which they had largely spun for themselves, but in which Joffre had intended to entrap them, ever since he had awakened to the true bent of their manœuvres.

September 3rd was the day. The German Supreme Command, now a little nearer to the front, having moved from Coblenz to Luxemburg, but still much too far away to be able to control the fighting, gave its blessing to the movements of the First and Second Armies. The Second Army reported that the French were retiring in complete disorder, basing this information, no doubt, on the stragglers and débris which it encountered in its advance. Von Kluck was placed in a dilemma by a Supreme Command Order that the First Army should echelon itself *behind* the Second. Was he to halt and mark time until von Bülow caught up with him? He decided that this was out of the question, and told the Supreme Command that he proposed to continue his advance south-eastwards, in accordance with their instructions to drive the French Army away from Paris. All through the day, the columns of the First Army pursued this manœuvre. They clashed with the left flank of the 5th Army, and gave it a rough handling. General Conneau's new Cavalry Corps was vigorously engaged. As the day wore on, no less than four German Corps began to converge on Château Thierry. The threat to the 5th Army became acute; but within it lay, at last, the opportunity for the riposte against the exposed flank of the enemy which Joffre had began to work for nine days previously.

It was an anxious day for the 5th Army, exhausting for the soldiers, difficult for the Staffs. A typical problem was the shortage of maps. As the French Armies retreated further and further into France, they became acutely embarrassed by the lack of military maps in anything like sufficient quantities for the needs of all units. The cartographers worked furiously to overcome the deficiency; meanwhile stacks of maps of Germany lay unused in vaults. They would never be required in that war.

The Foch detachment on the right of the 5th Army was still falling back, out of touch with the enemy, and trying to reorganise itself while it marched. On the left, the B.E.F. completed its retirement over the Marne without trouble. To the left again, the 6th

Army, now grouped inside the defensive system of Paris, had a quiet day. General Galliéni remained very worried; he pointed out to Joffre the impossibility of using the Territorial divisions of the garrison for field manœuvres; he asked urgently for instructions about the projected use of the forces under him; he also warned Joffre that the civil population, now that the Government had left, was disturbed, and needed feeding with any useful and encouraging news that might be available. Joffre saw his points. Before he could reply to them, however, Galliéni himself had learned that the German movements during the day had carried them away from the front of the 6th Army. (Indeed, G.H.Q. reported at 5 p.m. that the front of the B.E.F. was also clear of the enemy.) With creditable military instinct, Galliéni anticipated by several hours the orders that Joffre was preparing for him. He halted the retirement of the 6th Army. This was a turning point: it was the first positive preliminary move in the counterstroke.

As the realisation solidified within him that the crisis of the campaign was at hand, a painful necessity forced itself upon General Joffre. "In anticipation of the attack I was preparing and which would exact of everybody, commanders and troops alike, the maximum of will-power and tenacity, I passed in mental review all the chiefs who would be called upon to play a decisive part in the action." Doubt centred upon General Lanrezac. Ever since the Battle of Guise—in which he had done splendidly, once free of responsibility—Joffre says: ". . . the commander of the 5th Army had never ceased to discuss the orders given him and to raise objections to everything. His physical fatigue had intensified a tendency to criticise, which had always been one of the marked characteristics of his nature. He had become hesitating and timorous. Under the effects of his weakening authority, the staff of the 5th Army had become profoundly shaken, while his unpleasant relations with Sir John French had compromised the co-operation of the British Army with our own."

It was hardly possible to doubt what needed to be done. Yet Joffre shrank from the unpleasant task. "I could not help thinking of Lanrezac's brilliant career in time of peace. . . . It was precisely because I had the highest opinion of his intelligence that I had been the artisan of his military fortunes, and it was due to me that he now found himself at the head of that one of our armies which was the most difficult and delicate to command. But, in comparing what I had expected of him before this war broke out with the way he had acted in the presence of its stern realities, I was obliged to conclude, in spite of the genuine feeling I had for him, that his responsibilities had overwhelmed him. . . . What, then, was my duty? However painful it might be, however great my repugnance . . . I felt that another man had to be placed at the head of the 5th Army, if I wished to start the new offensive with the conviction that I had done everything in my power to ensure its success."

One further reassurance was needed before Joffre could take action: who would be Lanrezac's successor? The obvious candidate was Franchet d'Esperey. Joffre called on him, before going to see Lanrezac. He asked d'Esperey: "Do you feel yourself up to commanding an army?" "The same as another," replied the commander of the I Army Corps. That cryptic reply, half modest, half self-confident, settled the matter. D'Esperey was on his way to a marshal's baton; Lanrezac was on his way to Limoges, where the failures of the French Army spent their declining years grumbling to each other, and playing bridge.

"Every detail of those closing hours of the afternoon of September 3rd has remained graven in my memory," says Joffre. And yet the outlines of the scene at Lanrezac's headquarters, when the two men met, remain blurred. Joffre's account differs from Lanrezac's; Spears, who was a spectator, differs from both. Joffre says he went into Lanrezac's office: "Our talk was very short. 'My friend,' I said, 'you know how I have always aided you and helped to advance you in your career. But you are used up, undecided; you will have to give up the command of the 5th Army. I hate to tell you this, but I have to.'

"Lanrezac thought a moment and then answered: 'General, you are right'; and contrary to what I expected, he seemed like a man relieved from an overwhelming burden, for his whole face literally brightened."

Spears remembers it differently; he recalls the two generals walking up and down the playground of the school in which Fifth Army headquarters were lodged. "General Lanrezac was obviously dispirited and depressed. He talked a good deal and interrupted his walk now and then to make a point, but did not look at the Commander-in-Chief, and it was evident that the vigour he generally displayed in conversation was absent. His arms hung limp, he made no gestures except for an occasional movement of his hands.

"General Joffre appeared to be talking a little more than was his habit, but even this unusual effort on his part did not amount to saying more than a few sentences. At first he seemed to be speaking emphatically, then, after long silences, to be remonstrating gently. One gathered he might be saying: 'No, it is not as bad as that.'

"How the news got about I do not know, but the whisper passed round: 'The Commander-in-Chief is dismissing the General.'

"For some time such a possibility had been in the air, and now the moment had come the atmosphere was electric.

"The two big stout men, one fresh-coloured and calm, the other grey and haggard, continued to walk up and down, up and down. If the Commander-in-Chief was really dismissing Lanrezac his manner appeared to be very soothing and fatherly now.

"I have no idea how long the scene lasted. It may have been short, but it appeared to be endless, every moment weighed down by the fate of the coming battle.

"Suddenly the two generals disappeared. . . . I never saw General Lanrezac again. . . ."

It was the end, and a tragic one for an officer whose promise had been so great, and whose Army now, after dreadful tribulations, was about to reap the reward of its endurance. Joffre himself remarks: "Perhaps in a successful war Lanrezac might have accomplished marvels." Certainly, in his broad strategic assessments, he had often been right when G.Q.G. was wrong. But he had allowed his critical faculties to swamp his capacity for command. Spears, who saw him at close quarters through all this time, says: "the constant factor, the trait that emerges constantly in the story of the retreat of the 5th Army, is the reluctance of its commander to fight. . . . Not once of his own volition did he turn on the enemy between the Sambre and the Seine." Lanrezac had never had any faith in his Allies; by the time the Retreat ended, he had also lost faith in his own Army, and in the French leadership. Joffre was certainly right to part with him. He had done much mischief; but, at this distance, it is not becoming to be too hard upon him. He had borne a terrible burden; above all, at times, the burden of perceiving the truth, and not knowing how to act on it. The stress of high command in war upon a serious nature has not been sufficiently recognised, nor the value of those rare individuals who can go to sleep upon a decision, once taken, with untroubled minds.

10

The Counterstroke

IT WAS TIME for the Retreat to end. On September 4th, a Royal Field Artillery officer asked two of his sergeants: " 'Give a guess how long we have been out here?'

"They thought for a few minutes. 'Six weeks,' they said; 'perhaps seven.'

"And, you see, it was only a fortnight after all. But they would not believe it until a calendar was produced. Unconsciously everyone reckoned each night as another day, for nights and days were alike so far as work was concerned."

Even in this highly disciplined Expeditionary Force, the conditions under which the Retreat had to be carried out were beginning to tell. The dispersion of units, the losses among regimental officers and N.C.O.s, coupled with the general abandonment of the countryside by the civil population, created temptations which were not always overcome. In the deserted villages, it was easy to break into houses, perhaps only in order to use them as resting places; but the sight of valuables and household goods of all descriptions proved to be more than some of the soldiers could resist. It seemed a pity to leave everything for the Germans. General Smith-Dorrien recorded: ". . . a good many cases of unnecessary straggling and looting have taken place. Five men are to be tried by court-martial this evening."

Smith-Dorrien added that one-third of his Corps was still missing on this day; battle casualties accounted for by far the greater proportion of the loss, the rest consisted of the detached parties and the individual stragglers. Some of these men had astonishing adventures; some even remained in hiding in enemy territory until the very end of the war; others, when caught, and facing the death penalty which the rigours of German Military Occupation imposed, behaved with courage at least equal to that shown by their comrades in battle. Others, again, were different. Sir Philip Gibbs, then a war correspondent, wrote:

> "Was it any wonder that some of these young men who had laughed on the way to Waterloo Station, and held their heads high in the admiring gaze of London crowds, sure of their own heroism, slunk now in the backyards of French farmhouses, hid behind hedges when men in khaki passed, and told wild, incoherent tales, when cornered at last by some cold-eyed officer in some town of France to which they had blundered? It was the coward's chance, and I for one can hardly bring myself to blame the poor devil I met one day in Rouen, stuttering out lies to save his skin, or the two gunners, disguised in civil clothes, who begged from me near Amiens, or any of the half-starved stragglers who had 'lost' their regiments and did not go to find them."

There were some cavalry skirmishes again on September 4th, and the I Corps continued its retirement. The II and III Corps had a day of rest, and the Commander-in-Chief took the opportunity of visiting many units. As it turned out, his absence from G.H.Q. was unfortunate. But visiting the troops was one of the things that French did best, and no doubt his words to them, full of the admiration and gratitude that he sincerely felt, cheered them, and heartened them for the new struggles ahead.

Elsewhere, another commander was also making a personal impact. General Franchet d'Esperey was receiving the Staff of the 5th Army. "I wager," says Spears, "the war was not long enough to allow any of those who met the General that morning to forget the galvanic shock he gave them." There was to be no weakness whatsoever, d'Esperey told his officers. Any slackness, any dereliction of duty among the troops would be punished with the extreme penalty. Was he, then, to adopt a different standard for officers— above all Staff Officers? Certainly not. Anyone who failed in his duty would be shot. "It was easy to see from the faces of the officers as they streamed out of the Army Commander's room that they knew he meant every word he said. A certain rather stout lieutenant-colonel who had come in for d'Esperey's unfavourable notice looked as if he had fallen down several flights of stairs." At heart, d'Esperey was an amiable, courteous, jovial man; but he made it a deliberate policy, in this stark emergency of the war, to put his natural kindliness aside, and impel his despondent Army forward by methods which amounted to a reign of terror. They were justified by the changed demeanour of the Army from this day on—and by its success.

The first two major steps taken by d'Esperey on assuming his new command were characteristic. He made yet another change in the senior command of the Army, and then, in marked contrast to Lanrezac, turned his attention to his Allies. That very morning he set off to meet Sir John French. On his way, he received a message from Joffre, saying that the moment of decision was at hand; it might be the next day—would the 5th Army be ready to take part in the counter-attack? Before he could answer, d'Esperey would have to know what the British intended.

The sequence of accidents, which so often seems to be the mainspring of war, now multiplied. To save time, Franchet d'Esperey had arranged to meet French, not at his General Headquarters at Melun, but at Bray-sur-Seine. Simultaneously, General Galliéni perceived the imminence of the decisive moment, and went with General Maunoury to Melun. But neither Galliéni nor Franchet d'Esperey actually met French, who, as we have seen, was with his soldiers. Galliéni met Murray, and d'Esperey met Wilson. Out of the two meetings, two plans emerged which, while both containing the same central idea of an early counterstroke against the German right flank, differed in significant detail. Meanwhile, far away at G.Q.G., General Joffre and his Staff were also regarding the problem intently, in the light of the very full information that was coming in throughout the day about the passage of the German First Army across the Paris defences. As each item of news arrived—and the Royal Flying Corps by itself kept track of every Corps of the First Army—the positions of the enemy were marked on a large map. "The situation," says Joffre, "was impressive." Indeed it was; the whole of the German right wing had now thrust itself into the arc of a vast circle, with the French 6th Army on one side of it, the 3rd and 4th Armies on the other, the 5th and 9th Armies and the B.E.F. at the base. The time, Joffre decided, had come.

Berthelot disagreed; in the long discussion that followed, he argued that the Allied Armies needed several more days in which to prepare themselves for the counter-offensive, and that during these days the enemy would "entangle themselves more deeply in the net". Berthelot also clung to the idea that the main offensive, when it started, should be by the 5th Army and Foch's detachment—now called the 9th Army—striking in a north-westward direction. The argument was still in progress when a message came through from Galliéni, who was proposing to set the 6th Army in motion at once towards the east. He wanted to know whether Joffre would prefer it to operate on the north or the south bank of the River Marne. Joffre approved the movement, and, on Berthelot's insistence, told Galliéni that the 6th Army should advance along the the south bank. This reply formed the basis of Galliéni's discussions with Murray.

The heat was overpowering; tension, excitement and anxiety grew at G.Q.G., as Joffre and his Staff awaited the outcome of the two key consultations with French. Not all the news that came in while they waited was reassuring. The German First Army was across the Marne at Château Thierry, again threatening the left of the 5th Army; far away to the east, their Sixth Army was renewing its onslaught in Lorraine. It was late in the afternoon before the long-awaited reports began to come in, the first of them from Huguet, saying that French (actually it was Murray) had agreed to stand on his present position, and co-operate with either the 6th or the 5th Army, or both, as the occasion required. Joffre breathed a sigh of relief. Shortly afterwards another message came in, this time from Foch, who announced that he was ready to attack. There only remained Franchet d'Esperey. But Joffre's mind was now made up, and he directed Gamelin to draft orders for a general offensive on the 7th; the extra day partly met Berthelot's objections, and gave more time for co-ordination all round.

It was about 6.30 in the evening, and Joffre was just finishing his dinner, when Franchet d'Esperey reported. His plan, as agreed with Wilson and tersely summed up in two short notes, was of a very different calibre from Galliéni's. D'Esperey thought like a field commander; Galliéni was still very much the Military Governor of Paris. While Galliéni confined himself to discussing the manœuvres of the two Armies in his immediate vicinity—the 6th and the B.E.F.—d'Esperey, despite the fact that he had held his high command for less than twenty-four hours, did not hesitate to prescribe a large action involving three Armies besides his own. His ideas were simple, forthright, and comprehensive. His own Army would retire just far enough to bring it into line with the British; the British would pivot round to face eastward on his left; on their left the 6th Army would make a wide wheel to cover the British and strike in at the German rear; on the right, Foch's 9th Army would cover the flank of the 5th and menace the German left. All would advance concentrically towards the Marne. "My army can fight on the 6th," added d'Esperey, "but its condition is far from brilliant."

Joffre was delighted with d'Esperey's two notes. "They reflect," he says, "the greatest honour upon their author. Twenty-four hours before, Franchet d'Esperey had taken command of an army in full retreat and considerably shaken. It was only natural for him to fear that the fighting capacity of these troops . . . was at a very low ebb. But with the intelligent audacity which is found only in the souls of great leaders, Franchet d'Esperey splendidly seized the situation and did not hesitate to answer 'Yes' to a question which would have caused most men to flinch. I could not help thinking that if his predecessor had still been at the head of the 5th Army, the answer I had just received would probably have been quite different." Joffre adopted d'Esperey's plan, lock, stock and barrel, and it thereupon became the basis of his *Instruction Générale No. 6*, the Order that began the Battle of the Marne.

There were, however, two significant points arising. First, there was the question of the date. With Maunoury already on the move, and both d'Esperey and Foch willing to march on the 6th, Joffre somewhat unwillingly brought forward the day of battle. He remained convinced ever afterwards that "if it had been possible to put off the battle until the 7th, its results would have been considerably greater". But it is rarely feasible in war to tailor events exactly to one's fashion. There remained, also, the matter of the 6th Army's line of march, north or south of the Marne. Joffre told Galliéni that his new orders would now require Maunoury to advance along the north bank. What he did not realise was that Sir John French, returning to his headquarters, had issued orders to the B.E.F. on the basis of the Murray-Galliéni conversation, not knowing how very much more important the Wilson-d'Esperey discussion would prove to be—not knowing, indeed, what its outcome had been. And Murray and Galliéni, thinking in terms of the 6th Army acting south of the Marne, had agreed that the B.E.F. should retire one march further, to make room for the French to deploy. This march was already begun before the mistake was realised. Nobody can be blamed. It is amazing how much was accomplished during these crowded hours. But the effect of the B.E.F.'s last withdrawal on the 5th was to pull it some 15 miles further back than Joffre intended, to reduce its effectiveness in the initial stages of the Battle of the Marne, and to cause yet more distrust of the British among French officers.

All this emerged next day; but already, before September 4th had drawn to a close, Joffre was aware that some misunderstanding had occurred. Huguet informed him by telegram that Sir John French did not consider himself fully committed by the promises of his Staff Officers, and intended to study the whole question again, before finally deciding whether to join in the counter-offensive. There was only one thing to be done: in the middle of the night Joffre sent off a liaison officer, Major de Galbert, to G.H.Q., to urge upon French the capital importance of the plan.

At Supreme Headquarters von Moltke, too, had come to a decision. His frame of mind was no longer that of the optimistic communiqués which the Supreme Command had been circulating during the last few days. The Foreign Secretary, Herr Helfferich, met him on September 4th, and recorded: "I found Generaloberst von Moltke by no means in a cheerful mood inspired by victory; he was serious and depressed. He confirmed that our advanced troops were only 30 miles from Paris, 'but,' he added, 'we must not deceive ourselves. We have had successes, but we have not yet had victory. Victory means annihilation of the enemy's power of resistance. When armies of millions of men are opposed, the victor has prisoners. Where are ours? . . . The hardest work is still to be done.'"

That evening, von Moltke issued a new memorandum and new orders to all the Armies. The memorandum showed that he had, at any rate, begun to understand what was going on at the front, though the orders contributed nothing to the solution of their problems. The memorandum began:

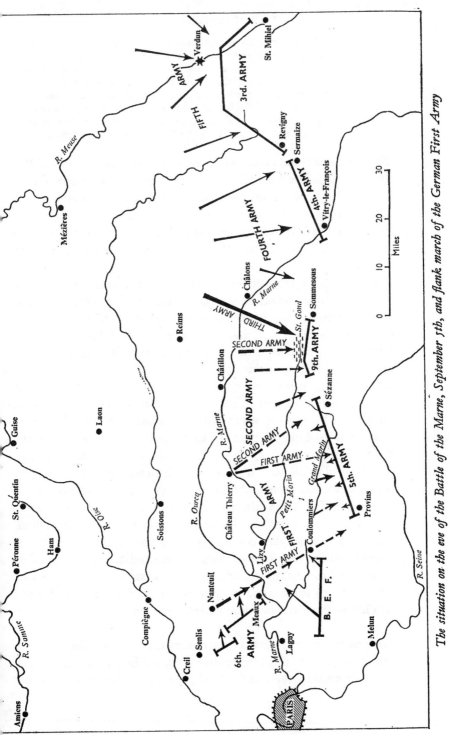

The situation on the eve of the Battle of the Marne, September 5th, and flank march of the German First Army

"The enemy has evaded the enveloping attack of the First and Second Armies, and a part of his forces has joined up with those about Paris. . . . The attempt to force the whole French Army back . . . towards the Swiss frontier is thus rendered impracticable, and the new situation to be appreciated shows that the enemy is bringing up new formations and concentrating superior forces in the neighbourhood of Paris, to protect the capital and to threaten the right flank of the German Army."

This, of course, was exactly true, and one would have supposed that the ensuing orders would have contained drastic instructions for the safeguarding of the threatened flank. Instead, the First and Second Armies were merely ordered to "remain facing the east front of Paris. Their task is to act against any operations of the enemy from the neighbourhood of Paris and to give each other mutual support to this end."

Von Moltke's real attention was still, despite his correct reading of the developments on his right, largely directed upon Lorraine. There, the Sixth and Seventh Armies were ordered to "continue to hold the enemy in position . . . but . . . take the offensive as soon as possible . . . "—a turn of phrase which blithely ignored the fact that they were already, this day, launched into another all-out attack upon de Castelnau's positions around Nancy. The Armies of the centre, the Fourth and Fifth, were ordered to assist this stroke on the left by pushing south-eastwards round Verdun. The Third Army was to hold itself ready to support either the left or the right wing, according to circumstance. What all this amounted to was the final manifestation of the idea which had never been very far from von Moltke's mind, of fighting two decisive battles at once, one as prescribed by the Schlieffen Plan, on the right, and the other in Lorraine. Even when the Battle of the Marne burst upon him, fraught with all its dire consequences, he continued to cherish this Lorraine offensive, although, against the stubborn resistance of de Castelnau's 2nd Army, it made no progress at all. From September 5th to 8th no further orders were issued to the First and Second Armies by the German Supreme Headquarters.

The final march of the B.E.F. was completed without difficulty in the continuing heat of this long summer. The soldiers were showing the strain of keeping their backs to the enemy. During these last few days, says Charteris, "they were very glum, they marched silently, doggedly, never a whistle or a song, or even a ribald jest, to help weary feet along the road. Staff Officers moving up and down the line with orders were glowered at gloomily. . . ." By nightfall, the whole Army had reached its halting-places, south-east of Paris, 166 miles from Mons, as the crow flies, but nearer 200, as the men had marched. It was calculated that, during the thirteen days of the Retreat, mounted men had averaged some three hours rest out of every twenty-four, infantry perhaps four hours. "I would never have believed," said one officer, "that men could be so tired and so hungry and yet live." And now, though the men in the ranks did not know it, as they stumbled into their billets, the Retreat was ended. The line they reached—incorrect, because of the misunderstanding produced by "too many cooks" the day before—was the line from which they would turn and attack the enemy: the Cavalry Division was concentrated on the right, feeling out towards the French Cavalry Corps which filled the 14-mile gap between the B.E.F. and the French 5th Army; then came the I Corps, tired, but almost intact; in the centre was the much-reduced II Corps; on the left was the incomplete III Corps. While they were all performing their last withdrawal, their Commander-in-Chief, at Melun, was holding another historic meeting.

Joffre's account of this day is somewhat misleading. We have seen that he went to bed full of anxiety about British intentions. Early on the 5th, however, his doubts were dispelled by a telephone message from Huguet which informed him: "The Marshal is going to conform to the intentions expressed in Order No. 6 of the G.Q.G., but by reason of the withdrawal carried out last night *with the object of leaving more room for the 6th Army to debouch south of the Marne** . . . the British Army will be in position facing east but a little to the rear of the line at first assigned to it." Joffre replied immediately: "General Joffre is leaving for Melun, where he will arrive about 2 p.m. He wishes to make a point of going personally to thank Marshal French for the decision he has taken." It is odd that he should have written afterwards that he went to Melun because his liaison officer, de Galbert, considered his mission to have failed, and told Joffre that "no one except myself could possibly succeed in obtaining a change

* NOTE: Author's italics.

in the attitude of the British Commander-in-Chief". Evidently the memory of evil times, the persistence of doubts once deeply felt, the recollection of continuing misunderstandings, overlaid all else in his mind. His account of what followed is therefore not to be taken literally, although its conclusion is valid enough. Fortunately, Spears, with his uncanny knack of being present at large occasions, witnessed the meeting.

Everyone stood: Sir John French, with Murray and Wilson beside him; Joffre put his cap on the table and faced French. "At once he began to speak in that low, toneless, albino voice of his, saying he had felt it his duty to come to thank Sir John personally for having taken a decision on which the fate of Europe might well depend. Sir John bowed. Then, without hurry or emphasis, Joffre explained the situation, developing the story of the German advance, and the change of direction of the First German Army. . . .

"We hung on his every word. We saw as he evoked it the immense battlefield over which the corps, drawn by the magnet of his will, were moving like pieces of intricate machinery, until they clicked into their appointed places. . . .

"Joffre was now foretelling what would happen on the morrow and on the day after and on the day after that, and as a prophet he was heard with absolute faith. We were listening to the story of the victory of the Marne, and we absolutely believed."

Joffre expounded his plan. He spoke of the British role, asking for the total support of the British Army. "Then, turning full on Sir John, with an appeal so intense as to be irresistible, clasping both his own hands so as to hurt them, General Joffre said:

" 'Monsieur le Maréchal, c'est la France qui vous supplie.'

"His hands fell to his sides wearily. The effort he had made had exhausted him.

"We all looked at Sir John. He had understood and was under the stress of strong emotion. Tears stood in his eyes, welled over and rolled down his cheeks.

"He tried to say something in French. For a moment he struggled with his feelings and with the language, then turning to an English officer . . . who stood beside him, he exclaimed: 'Damn it, I can't explain. Tell him that all that men can do our fellows will do.' "

It was an instant in which two men met, not with their minds

alone, nor with their feelings alone, but with their whole beings.
Joffre says: "I had distinctly felt the emotion which seemed to grip
the British Commander-in-Chief; above all I had remarked the tone
of his voice, and I felt, as did all the witnesses to the scene, that these
simple words were equivalent to an agreement signed and sworn
to." If great leadership does not lie in the capacity to capture the
imagination of men—men, in this case, of another race—and produce
such an effect as this, then it is hard to see what meaning the words
contain.

Not even the anti-climax of Murray's swift and businesslike intervention with talk of timetables and marches could efface the impression of the scene. Not even the tea which, this being a British
headquarters, was then served, could alter its impact. There was no
question now that all the Allied armies would strike together.

Maunoury had struck already, along the Ourcq, driving into the
flank of the German columns which were still marching south-east
towards the Seine. Von Kluck had reported to the Supreme Command that he proposed to continue his advance, since otherwise the
initiative would be surrendered to the Allies. In the evening,
Colonel Hentsch, liaison officer from Supreme Headquarters,
arrived and told him of the situation on other Army fronts. Once
again the left wing had been held up at Nancy; the Fourth and Fifth
Armies were making only slow progress; the Supreme Command
recommended that the advance of the right wing should now be
stopped, but "at leisure", there was no need for "special haste". Not
until late that night did von Kluck learn that his right rear had been
attacked. The German IV Reserve Corps had put up a strong
resistance to Maunoury around St. Supplets, and the position of the
6th Army was by no means as good as its commander at first
reported; but from the German point of view, its very existence was
an omen of disaster.

Maunoury's attack on the Ourcq raised the curtain for the grand
action. The 5th Army reported: "All measures taken to attack
tomorrow . . ."; and Franchet d'Esperey told his troops: "It is
important that every soldier should know before the battle that the
honour of France and the salvation of the homeland depend upon
the energy he displays in tomorrow's fighting. The country relies

upon every man to do his duty." Joffre issued his Order of the Day:

> "At the moment when the battle upon which hangs the fate of the country is about to begin, all must remember that the time for looking back is past; every effort must be concentrated on attacking and throwing the enemy back.
>
> "Troops which can no longer advance must at any cost keep the ground that has been won, and must die where they stand rather than give way.
>
> "Under present conditions no weakness can be tolerated."

There would be no weakness. The intelligence of the French soldier is proverbial; he knew what was expected of him; he fully shared the determination of his leaders to hurl the invader back.

And all along the line of billets and bivouacs of the B.E.F. the orders for the next day's march were coming through. Where would it take them? In one weary battery of the II Corps, the general opinion favoured Paris.

"Just about 6 p.m. the major came into the lines with a paper in his hand. There was something in his walk, something about him—the men jumped up as he approached. 'Paris?'—the major shook his head. 'Not—not—is it advance, sir?' The major nodded. 'We are going to advance,' he said. . . .

"There was a cheer which must have startled the French Government in Bordeaux, or wherever they had gone to.

"The drivers rushed at their horses, the gunners rushed to the limbers to help hook in. . . . Another rousing shout, which soon merged into the cheery strains of 'All aboard for Dixie', and the battery began a march, this time in the right direction, which only stopped at 2 a.m. for the sake of the horses. The men were ready to go on for a week."

"The happiest day in my life; we marched towards the rising sun," wrote Colonel Seely, in his diary on the 6th. The whole B.E.F. shared this feeling of exultation; as the day proceeded, it grew, with the realisation that the Germans were now, in turn, retreating. The troops actually in touch with the enemy, particularly the cavalry, witnessed unforgettable sights. "My squadron was advanced guard," says Bridges, "and from the village of Peçy which was on a hill, we were able to see their infantry halted on the road. A Uhlan patrol which reconnoitred us was hotly dealt with. I sent back a frantic appeal for guns. A German battery barked at us and set fire to a house. Then the phenomenon occurred. Under our eyes the enemy column began to wheel round in the road and retire to the north. I saw an aeroplane being towed along the road turn round to be towed home. It was the peak of von Kluck's advance."

There was no doubt about it: the Germans were going back. Yet the advance was slow work. On the right, where several large forests lay in the path of Sir Douglas Haig's Corps, the British movements were especially deliberate. The Corps averaged no more than a 5-mile advance throughout the day. On the left, the II and II Corps were able to do better. They moved forward some 10 miles each, and at 11 p.m. that night the 1st Wiltshires, of the 3rd Division of the II Corps, forced the crossing of the Grand Morin. It was a proud moment for General Smith-Dorrien. His Corps, which had had all the hardest fighting, and the severest loss during the Retreat, was nevertheless leading the whole Army in the counter-attack.

The Battle of the Marne lasted for four days. Shifting, swaying, confused, nowhere, and at no time, did it present the traditional aspect of victory. There was no panic rout of an Army, rushing from a stricken field, as at Waterloo; there was no interviewing of the beaten general by the victor, and laying down of arms, as at Appomattox Court House. There was no wholesale punishment of the defeated, as in the Falaise Gap. It must be said that Generals von Kluck and von Bülow, once they realised what had befallen them, extracted their armies with great skill from the snare that Joffre had cast round them. The German soldier, in defeat, displayed all that courage and patient tenacity which, in the Second World War, enabled him to fight on after Stalingrad and the crushing disaster in Normandy. In September 1914, with all his high hopes suddenly cast down, with all his huge exertions brought to nought, he showed in adversity the qualities that were to make the rest of the War into a terrible martyrdom.

Maunoury's Army, which should have struck into the German rear and completed their discomfiture, was stopped in its tracks on the second day of the battle, and, indeed, had to stand on the defensive for the greater part of it. Foch's Army was for a time so hard pressed that, but for the indomitable will of its commander, it might have had to retreat again. But, as the two German Armies reacted violently and stubbornly to these threats against their outer flanks, a gap widened between them. It was the advance of the 5th Army and the B.E.F. into this gap that made the Battle of the Marne a decisive battle of the War, and forced the Germans back to the line of the River Aisne. The front formed along this line scarcely shifted during the next four years. Since August 29th, when the 5th Army fought the Battle of Guise, and, for the British, since Le Cateau on August 26th, the campaign had been conducted by the soldiers mainly with their feet, and the decisive point had always been inside the minds of the generals. When the Allies reached the Aisne, a process began which was to turn the war on the Western Front, until 1918, into one long soldiers' battle, nullifying, time after time, every effort that the generals made.

In this short period, while generalship in its established style continued to dominate the field of battle, reputations came and went. When it was understood that a great and lasting victory had been won, there were naturally many claimants for the honour of having conceived it. Joffre, Galliéni, even Wilson, have all been put forward as the true architects of victory. Time has shown that the man mainly responsible was Joffre, rebuilding, brick by brick, upon the ruin of his first hopes. He did not suddenly dream up his great plan; it grew upon him, at first out of the simple need to have an army that he could command on his imperilled left flank. Out of that need, steadily, one might almost say inevitably, had grown all that followed. At the right time, Galliéni gave proof of his soldierly qualities by spontaneously initiating the very actions that Joffre required. But Joffre himself pays a typical generous tribute to a man who is now largely unknown, at any rate in England, but who ought to be remembered: "The role played by Franchet d'Esperey during the day of September 4th, 1914, deserves to be written large across the pages of history: it is he who made the Battle of the Marne possible."

What had been the contribution of the B.E.F.? In the later stages, it has to be admitted, it was largely a negative one. Uncertainty about British intentions, their apparent determination to do nothing but retreat while the Germans over-ran the greater part of northern France, added enormously to Joffre's difficulties. Kitchener's part in overcoming this tendency, no matter how distasteful it was to Sir

John French, had a value that should never be forgotten. But in the early fighting, at Mons, on the way to Le Cateau, and above all, at Le Cateau, the quality of this professional Army produced effects which, had they been matched at any other point of the Allied line, must have made the story very different. It is pointless to single out any arm for special praise; the infantry won glory that can never be taken from them; but the artillery and the cavalry also maintained standards almost unbelievably high. The rearward services, whose task is rarely easy, surpassed themselves.

On September 5th, the day before the first reinforcements arrived to refill the depleted ranks, 20,000 men were absent from their units in the B.E.F. Many of these, however, rejoined later. The final casualty returns for the Mons Campaign amounted to just over 15,000 men and officers killed, wounded and missing, and 42 guns lost. "Such a casualty list can," says the Official History, "in the circumstances, be only considered as astonishingly light. Its seriousness lay in the fact that, whether in guns or men, the loss had fallen almost wholly upon the left wing . . . and above all on the II Corps." The men who fought under General Smith-Dorrien earned something more than the handsome Mons Star which was later awarded to them; they earned recognition for one of the finest sustained endeavours in the Army's story.

After the first enthusiasm came the disappointment of Retreat; as the Retreat continued, deep gloom and despondency followed; then came the new advance, and all was splendour once more. The new enthusiasm was as infectious as the old, and time would show that it was just as dangerous. On September 13th, as the Allied Armies struggled without success on the rain-soaked slopes of the Aisne, just one week after the end of the long retreat, Wilson was talking to the French generals again:

"Berthelot asked me when I thought we should cross into Germany, and I replied that unless we made some serious blunder we ought to be at Elsenborn in four weeks. He thought three weeks."

APPENDIX

COMPOSITION OF THE B.E.F.
(and names of principal officers)

Commander-in-Chief: Field-Marshal Sir J. D. P. French, G.C.B., G.C.V.O., K.C.M.G.
Chief of the General Staff: Lieut.-Gen. Sir A. J. Murray, K.C.B., C.V.O., D.S.O.
Major-General, General Staff: Maj.-Gen. H. H. Wilson, C.B., D.S.O.
G.S.O.1 (Intelligence): Colonel G. M. W. Macdonogh
Quartermaster-General: Maj.-Gen. Sir W. R. Robertson, K.C.V.O., C.B., D.S.O.

The Cavalry Division
G.O.C.: Maj.-Gen. E. H. Allenby, C.B.

1st Cavalry Brigade:
G.O.C.: Brig.-Gen. C. J. Briggs, C.B.
2nd Dragoon Guards (Queen's Bays)
5th Dragoon Guards
11th Hussars

2nd Cavalry Brigade:
G.O.C.: Brig.-Gen. H. de B. de Lisle, C.B., D.S.O.
4th Dragoon Guards
9th Lancers
18th Hussars

3rd Cavalry Brigade:
G.O.C.: Brig.-Gen. H. de la P. Gough, C.B.
4th Hussars
5th Lancers
16th Lancers

4th Cavalry Brigade:
G.O.C.: Brig.-Gen. Hon. C. E. Bingham, C.V.O., C.B.
Household Cavalry Regiment
6th Dragoon Guards (Carabiniers)
3rd Hussars

5th Cavalry Brigade:
G.O.C.: Brig.-Gen. Sir P. W. Chetwode, Bart., D.S.O.

2nd Dragoons (Royal Scots Greys)
12th Lancers
20th Hussars
"D", "E", "I", "J", "L" Batteries, R.H.A.

I. Corps:

G.O.C.: Lieut.-Gen. Sir D. Haig, K.C.B., K.C.I.E., K.C.V.O., A.D.C.-Gen.
B.G.G.S.: Brig.-Gen. J. E. Gough, V.C., C.M.G., A.D.C.

1st Division:
G.O.C.: Maj.-Gen. S. H. Lomax

1st (Guards) Bgde.:
G.O.C.: Brig.-Gen. F. I. Maxse, C.V.O., C.B., D.S.O.
1/Coldstream Guards
1/Scots Guards
1/Black Watch
2/Royal Munster Fusiliers

2nd Bgde.:
G.O.C.: Brig.-Gen. E. S. Bulfin, C.V.O., C.B.
2/Royal Sussex Regiment
1/Loyal North Lancashire Regiment
1/Northamptonshire Regiment
2/King's Royal Rifle Corps

APPENDIX

3rd Bgde.:

G.O.C.: Brig.-Gen. H. J. S. Landon, C.B.
1/Queen's (Royal West Surrey Regiment)
1/South Wales Borderers
1/Gloucestershire Regiment
2/Welch Regiment
"A" Squadron, 15th Hussars
XXV, XXVI, XXXIX, XLIII Bgdes., R.F.A.;
26th Heavy Battery, R.G.A.
23rd, 26th Field Companies, R.E.

2nd Division:

G.O.C.: Maj.-Gen. C. C. Monro, C.B.

4th (Guards) Bgde.:	*5th Bgde.:*
G.O.C.: Brig.-Gen. R. Scott-Kerr, C.B., M.V.O., D.S.O.	G.O.C.: Brig.-Gen. R. C. B. Haking, C.B.
2/Grenadier Guards	2/Worcestershire Regiment
2/Coldstream Guards	2/Oxfordshire & Buckinghamshire Light Infantry
3/Coldstream Guards	2/Highland Light Infantry
1/Irish Guards	2/Connaught Rangers

6th Bgde.:

G.O.C.: Brig.-Gen. R. H. Davies, C.B. (N.Z. Staff Corps)
1/King's (Liverpool Regiment)   1/Royal Berkshire Regiment
2/South Staffordshire Regiment   1/King's Royal Rifle Corps
"B" Squadron, 15th Hussars
XXXIV, XXXVI, XLI, XLIV Bgdes., R.F.A.;
35th Heavy Battery, R.G.A.
5th, 11th Field Companies, R.E.

II Corps:

G.O.C.: Lieut.-Gen. Sir J. M. Grierson, K.C.B., C.V.O., C.M.G., A.D.C.-Gen.
General Sir H. L. Smith-Dorrien, G.C.B., D.S.O.
B.G.G.S.: Brig.-Gen. G. T. Forestier-Walker, A.D.C.

3rd Division:

G.O.C.: Maj.-Gen. H. I. W. Hamilton, C.V.O., C.B., D.S.O.

7th Bgde.:	*8th Bgde.:*
G.O.C.: Brig.-Gen. F. W. N. Mc-Cracken, C.B., D.S.O.	G.O.C.: Brig.-Gen. B. J. C. Doran, C.B.
3/Worcestershire Regiment	2/Royal Scots
2/South Lancashire Regiment	2/Royal Irish Regiment
1/Wiltshire Regiment	4/Middlesex Regiment
2/Royal Irish Rifles	1/Gordon Highlanders

9th Bgde.:

G.O.C.: Brig.-Gen. F. C. Shaw, C.B.
1/Northumberland Fusiliers   1/Lincolnshire Regiment
4/Royal Fusiliers   1/Royal Scots Fusiliers
"C" Squadron, 15th Hussars
XXIII, XL, XLII, XXX Bgdes., R.F.A.;
48th Heavy Battery, R.G.A.
56th, 57th Field Companies, R.E.

5th Division:
G.O.C.: Maj.-Gen. Sir C. Fergusson, Bart., C.B., M.V.O., D.S.O.

13th Bgde.:
G.O.C.: Brig.-Gen. G. J. Cuthbert, C.B.
2/King's Own Scottish Borderers
2/Duke of Wellington's (West Riding Regiment)
1/Queen's Own (Royal West Kent Regiment)
2/King's Own (Yorkshire Light Infantry)

14th Bgde.:
G.O.C.: Brig.-Gen. S. P. Rolt, C.B.
2/Suffolk Regiment
1/East Surrey Regiment
1/Duke of Cornwall's Light Infantry
2/Manchester Regiment

15th Bgde:
G.O.C.: Brig.-Gen. A. E. W. Count Gleichen, K.C.V.O., C.B., C.M.G., D.S.O.
1/Norfolk Regiment
1/Bedfordshire Regiment
1/Cheshire Regiment
1/Dorsetshire Regiment
"A" Squadron, 19th Hussars
XV, XXVII, XXVIII, VIII Bgdes., R.F.A.;
108th Heavy Battery, R.G.A.
17th, 59th Field Companies, R.E.

III Corps:
G.O.C.: Maj.-Gen. W. P. Pulteney, C.B., D.S.O.
B.G.G.S.: Brig.-Gen. J. P. Du Cane, C.B.

4th Division:
G.O.C.: Maj.-Gen. T. D'O. Snow, C.B.

10th Bgde.:
G.O.C.: Brig.-Gen. J. A. L. Haldane, C.B., D.S.O.
1/Royal Warwickshire Regiment
2/Seaforth Highlanders
1/Royal Irish Fusiliers
2/Royal Dublin Fusiliers

11th Bgde.:
G.O.C.: Brig.-Gen. A. G. Hunter-Weston, C.B., D.S.O.
1/Somerset Light Infantry
1/East Lancashire Regiment
1/Hampshire Regiment
1/Rifle Brigade

12th Bgde.:
G.O.C.: Brig.-Gen. H. F. M. Wilson, C.B.
1/King's Own (Royal Lancaster Regiment)
2/Lancashire Fusiliers
2/Royal Inniskilling Fusiliers
2/Essex Regiment
"B" Squadron, 19th Hussars
XIV, XXIX, XXXII, XXXVII Bgdes., R.F.A.;
31st Heavy Battery, R.G.A.
7th, 9th Field Companies, R.E.

19th Bgde.:
G.O.C.: Maj.-Gen. L. G. Drummond, C.B., M.V.O.
2/Royal Welch Fusiliers
1/Cameronians
1/Middlesex Regiment
2/Argyll & Sutherland Highlanders

ROYAL FLYING CORPS:
G.O.C.: Brig.-Gen. Sir D. Henderson, K.C.B., D.S.O.

2nd Aeroplane Squadron
3rd Aeroplane Squadron
4th Aeroplane Squadron
5th Aeroplane Squadron
1st Aircraft Park